Peter Somerville-Large was born in 1928 and educated in Dublin. After a decade working abroad he returned to Ireland to take up a writing career. His many books of travel and social history include *The Grand Irish Tour*, *Irish Eccentrics* and *Cappaghglass*.

Praise for *An Irish Childhood*

'Somerville-Large, well known for his books of travel and social history, recalls in graphic detail the joys and tribulations of a childhood spent in a milieu that has vanished.'   *Books of Ireland*

'*An Irish Childhood*, beautifully and evocatively written, takes the reader back to the sensations and excitements of childhood, and paints the most vivid picture of a vanished world – at once so recent, yet so far away. An absorbing and memorable portrait of one man's childhood in pre-war Ireland.'   *Fast Forward*

AN IRISH CHILDHOOD

PETER SOMERVILLE-LARGE

Robinson
LONDON

Constable & Robinson Ltd
3 The Lanchesters
162 Fulham Palace Road
London W6 9ER
www.constablerobinson.com

First published in the UK by Constable,
an imprint of Constable & Robinson Ltd, 2002

This paperback edition published by Robinson,
an imprint of Constable and Robinson Ltd, 2003

A copy of the British Library Cataloguing in
Publication Data is available from the British Library.

ISBN 1-84119-708-4

Printed and bound in the EU

10 9 8 7 6 5 4 3 2 1

For Phil

Contents

Illustrations

1

Fitzwilliam Place

H<small>E WAS A</small> military man, well over six feet tall, with pale blue eyes and a huge snowy white moustache. On this Easter Sunday his tattoos were hidden by his clothes.

Last summer he had taken off his shirt and showed them to me. We were on the tennis court one warm afternoon when he turned round so that I could see the dragon on his back. He revealed the butterfly and dragonfly on his chest, the two snakes wriggling down each arm towards the giant centipede near his right wrist and the dead toad, belly turned upward and claws in the air, which lay across his left forearm. As long as he was alive the snake would be separated from the toad, like the lovers on Keats' Grecian urn.

Today he carried a magnificent large Easter egg, the decoration on its shining paper intricate as Fabergé with sprigs of flowers, rabbits and yellow chicks. It was for me, his godchild.

Watched by various relations, including my brother Phil, who I knew was sick with envy, I rushed forward to take my prize. Just as I got to Uncle Bris he raised his arms and dropped it. I began shrieking and he was howling with laughter as the egg lay splintered on the ground, a ruin of chocolate shards and torn silver paper.

I had failed miserably to achieve the right kind of careless indifference to the harsh arrows of misfortune I might receive over a lifetime. The laughter echoed after me as Nanny Somers rushed to take me away. What a bastard!

That was my Great Uncle Brisbane whose name I shared.

I was born in 1928, almost exactly five years before Uncle Bris dropped my Easter egg, in the appropriately named Hatch Street Nursing Home in Dublin where a good many Protestant babies saw the light of day. Sir John Hatch had laid out the street in the eighteenth century.

Ireland had been at peace for five years after the bloodshed of the Troubles and the Civil War. Although my family was Unionist, every member of it felt passionately Irish. My Uncle Paddy always expressed great sadness for those forced to live in England. 'Poor devil!' he would say about anyone who took the boat. The writer, Edith Somerville, known to us as Cousin Edith, once mused on our particular form of Irishness: 'I have a theory that living on the land, devouring its fruits and associating with the people of an adopted country creates a closer kinship than blood.'

In St Stephens, Upper Mount Street, the pepperpot church, I was christened Brisbane Peter. The name Brisbane came from our relations named Warren who had lived outside Cork city. Early in the nineteenth century the Warrens had sought to flatter a Scotsman named Thomas Brisbane by naming their sons after him. He had become a friend of theirs when he was in Cork as a young ensign in the 38th Regiment. Later on Thomas Brisbane became

Governor of New South Wales and a river and a small convict settlement to the north of the colony were named after him, as well as several members of my family. Long's *History of New South Wales* described Sir Thomas Brisbane as 'a man of the best intentions but disinclined to business and deficient in energy'.

My second name, by which, thank God, I was known, came from a West Highland white terrier who was buried at the back of our house in Fitzwilliam Place where his inscribed granite tombstone is there to this day.

'Peter was a lovely little dog,' my mother told me. 'You are very lucky to be called after him.'

My brother was called Philip after Uncle Phil who was Uncle Bris's brother. We were close in age and we used to chant: 'May came and Phil came; April came and Peter came!'

Until I was five years old we lived in Fitzwilliam Place where my father, Collis Somerville-Large, practised as a surgeon. Ireland might have gained its independence and the century might be in its third decade, but among the tranquil brick terraces around Fitzwilliam Square and Merrion Square life had hardly changed in a hundred years. They were still smart, unlike the streets just beyond the golden nucleus. The doggerel advice from one lady to another written at the beginning of the century held good:

> You had better beware, said she,
> For Merrion Square, said she,
> Won't sit down to supper
> With Baggot Street Upper.

Doctors and lawyers continued to have keys to the park in Fitzwilliam Square and share a quiet prosperity. Most were Protestant, prosperous people whom the Free State wished well after the discomforts of the Troubles. There were exceptions like the Hemphills at the end of the street who were Catholic and had their private chapel tacked on to their house, which today, I believe, is filled with computers.

Our house was part of a street containing the longest unbroken stretch of Georgian houses in Europe. If you stepped out on the pavement you could see a view of the Dublin Mountain and the Hellfire Club. Sixteen Fitzwilliam Place was five storeys high and, like a doll's house, each floor was a separate entity from the rest. They were linked by terrible stairs. The Georgians, and others in cities all over Europe, built their beautiful terraces with thoughtless cruelty when servants were plentiful. At the end of the seventeenth century out of a total adult population of 28,000, Dublin had 7,000 servants. By my parents' time their numbers had dwindled drastically, but Sixteen still had a cook and two maids, Mary and Margaret, shod in shoes that always squeaked, who were expected to make the regular climb up four flights from the basement to our nursery. Upstairs and downstairs was a synonym for torture.

For the rest of the time, when they were not bringing up food and coal to the top floor or answering bells that summoned them to the drawing room, or to the front door where some sick person waited, Mary and Margaret lived together with Ellen the cook in eternal gloom. The basement kitchen faced east, so that a thin shaft of sunlight filtered down from the street only on summer mornings. Nearly every house in the Place and Square had a similar

4

kitchen. Other cooks like Ellen presided over a large stove, polished black, whose burning coal made the atmosphere permanently grubby, producing cooling food to be carried by other maids, wearing similar caps and starched aprons, up the stone steps to the dining room.

Behind the kitchen were rooms that were darker still – a scullery with wooden dish rack and Belfast sink, now beloved by trendy architects, storerooms, with forgotten features like the wire meat safes, and dark bedrooms with bars on the windows. No wonder at the first true sign of democracy and prosperity in any country servants cease to be servants and leave their tormentors to do the washing up. A decade and the Emergency would pass before servants would flee their bondage from town houses and country houses all over Ireland. In country houses around the late forties and early fifties there was the great movement of Bringing Up the Kitchen as basements were abandoned to darkness and rats.

In the thirties most of the doctors who congregated around Fitzwilliam Square carried out part of their practice in their homes. On week days throughout certain hours of the afternoon my father's consulting rooms on the ground floor generated a certain amount of agitation. The doorbell rang or the lion-headed knocker was banged and footsteps or the thump of crutches on the parquet floor of the hall sounded up the stairwell as patients were guided past the brass drunkard's rail, polished like the knocker until it shone like pale gold, and shown into the waiting room.

At other times of day Sixteen functioned like an ordinary household. Mary or Margaret carried meals up from the kitchen to the dining room. For tea they had to go higher, fifty steps up to the the floor above, balancing loaded trays, the silver teapot spitting from its spout. Those waiting for tea and cucumber sandwiches, and little sponge cakes vaccinated with whipped cream and a dab of jam, and fruitcake which would keep hunger pangs at bay before dinner three hours later, sat in the drawing room with its fine Georgian proportions stretching across two bay windows and their useless little wrought-iron balconies.

When visitors came we would be sent down to the drawing room for inspection in the time-honoured Victorian way. My mother was an enthusiastic producer of amateur plays that took place in the large drawing room. For a very short time we were expected to take part.

'You needn't be shy – they are only friends.'

So I was dressed in a silk tunic and pixie hat in order to play one of Peter Pan's boy chums. Phil, who naturally played Peter, gave me a great push towards the hostile faces waiting to watch me.

'Look! His trousers are coming down!' Pitiful tears, as loud as those which I exhibited to Uncle Bris, put an end to my stage career.

Above the drawing room were bedrooms, and above them our nursery.

Our world was self-contained, and for much of the time what happened downstairs, the coming and going of patients and visitors and the movements of other members of the household, was none of our business. Perched under the roof at the top of the house, the nursery suite consisted of some low rooms cut off with a final curving flight behind a closed door so that we were out of sight and sound, like Mrs Rochester. In addition to a couple of bedrooms, a bathroom, a small kitchen where Nanny Somers cooked for us and saved Mary and Margaret many a climb, there was the large nursery itself, spanning the two top windows overlooking the street. The windows were barred; if ever there was a fire we would have had it.

A mahogany high chair with feeding tray was part of the furniture long after Phil and I ceased to use it. A long rattan-covered stool could be used as a boat when it was turned upside down. On the walls were depictions of HMS *Victory*, and the meeting of Wellington and Blücher after Waterloo. To some extent my parents maintained imperial links – they were invited to attend the coronation of King George VI and the motto of the Large family happens to be *Coronam Defendo* – but which of them chose these pictures? Neither would have been interested in Wellington's achievements, although my father had some things in common with Nelson – a love of sailing, a tendency to seasickness, and an ability to command. I think those prints, together with the sentimental picture of a goose girl, appeared on our walls out of indifference – anything would do for the top floor. But one picture we did like – Dürer's hare; I can remember every whisker.

The back windows of the nursery overlooked the Grand Canal; among the reeds long barges were still regularly pulled by hairy-hoofed horses and for all we knew they still went as far as Ballinasloe, as they had done in Thackeray's time. We could watch the barges slowly passing, beginning their uneventful passage into the heart of rural Ireland, the bargees smoking their pipes, the great Clydesdales straining against the long craft under the cool green trees.

The front windows overlooking Fitzwilliam Place were

more interesting. In the early morning we could hear the whistling of drovers and barking of dogs as cattle were driven down to the market and the boats. At other times we listened to the tinny music of a barrel organ or identified the horses and vans that clopped past. So much was still horse-drawn. Standing at the window looking down provided us with more amusement than the long sessions with the wooden box of bricks and the lead soldiers (little British soldiers in red coats).

Johnson, Mooney and O'Brien's tall bread van was painted rusty red. Who had written the doggerel chanted by every child in Dublin from the slums to the squares – 'Johnson, Mooney and O'Brien, bought a horse for one and nine'? The milkman's churns, ringed with polished brass, had bright taps through which the milk poured into jugs. Even in the 1930s the pasteurised milk that we drank was a middle-class luxury. As a surgeon having to operate on diseased bones, my father had particular insight into the horrors of TB.

The coal vans, with their sacks neatly arranged two by two, called regularly, as a succession of Dublin's Dolittles lifted the cast-iron cover and poured coal down the coal hole to feed the fires on every floor. That included the fire in our nursery, guarded by the tall fender hung with our socks and shirts. Every morning from November on we listened for Margaret panting as she heaved up the buckets from the basement.

Numerous laundry vans carried clean linen in brown paper parcels – the Metropolitan, the White Swan, the White Heather, the Court Laundry, pale and cream-coloured. The sides of the Swastika vans bore a startling good luck symbol, which did not yet have any sinister association. Perhaps the idea was brought back from India by someone with a colonial background. Even the laundry's yellow receipts, the emblem stamped against a black circle surrounded by lettering, SWASTIKA LAUNDRY LTD. BALLSBRIDGE, were as eye-catching as a flag at a Nuremberg rally.

When we peered straight down we could watch people on the pavement passing our front door. One day, when Nanny Somers was downstairs on some panting trip to the basement, Phil had an idea.

'Let's make rain.'

A tap and a jug contributed to a lovely game, as we went backwards and forwards to the window and through the bars threw down water four floors to the pavement, creating what was more a waterfall than the drizzle we intended. The third or fourth time we emptied the jug, the water fell on someone who received a full soaking shower. We looked out and saw that the man did not walk on, but turned at once and came up our steps, his clothes dripping. We heard the doorbell ring, followed by a very long silence, and then hasty footsteps on the little staircase outside the nursery. Our father was angry enough to leave a patient, probably half-encased in plaster of Paris, his arm or foot stretched out straight, to storm up three flights of stairs to beat us.

That was about the only time I remember him in the nursery. My mother ascended to our little apartment more often. On most evenings she turned up in our bedroom after we were clothed in thick striped Vyella prison outfits to hear us invoke God to bless all the relations as well as Nanny, Mary, Margaret and Cook. She also read to us; prayers and reading would be part of our evening routine long after we left Sixteen. She read us the story of Babar, the stylish French elephant, and the old lady with whom he had such a curious relationship. Little Black Sambo's parents, Black Mumbo and Black Jumbo, still not politically incorrect, were crude jolly smiling creations; the end of the predatory tigers, turned to pancakes and fried in ghee was satisfying. 'And little Black Sambo ate three hundred and sixty five because he was so hungry.' But why did we have to listen to *Struwwelpeter* and the other terrors created by internationally acclaimed Dr Hoffman in 1847 to amuse his own tough children and dream of the tailor leaping into the nursery aiming his huge scissors for the thumbs we furtively sucked?

Later horror would come from Edgar Allan Poe's *Tales of Mystery and Imagination*, illustrated by Harry Clarke with fevered consumptive intensity. The nightmare picture of the man in the ship's bunk who believes he is in a coffin has led me to leave instructions in my will to be cremated.

If books were not terrifying they tended to be the preferences of our elders who assumed they would amuse us. We heard the work of unhappy geniuses like Beatrix Potter and J. M. Barrie who had sublimated early miseries in worlds of fantasy superior to the real world imposed on children by grown-ups. Potter's animals inevitably appealed to my mother, while she was particularly fond of Peter Pan; she very much liked the idea of the Darling children having a nanny similar to Bruin, our old English sheepdog. Bruin's portrait had recently been painted by Phoebe Donovan, the artist who painted all the top dogs and horses in Ireland. No one painted our portraits.

We listened to the newly published *Mary Poppins*, about another remarkable children's nanny who also bore no comparison whatsoever to our whiskered old Nanny

Somers. The works of A. A. Milne, featuring his unhappy son, were another grown-up preference. I have read that when *When We Were Very Young* was first published, appreciation for this 'adorable nonsense' was almost universal; in America enthusiastic letters came from three Supreme Court justices, eleven rear-admirals, twelve major-generals, Fred Astaire and President Coolidge. In the Jaffa Chamber of Commerce busy Arab merchants took time off to recite endless repeats of 'Christopher Robin goes hoppity, hoppity hop.' We never cared for teddy bears.

I do not remember anything in the way of Empire literature – no *Our Ireland's Story* or *The Glories of Britain*. But when we went to school the history we would be taught was entirely English. We learned by rote the names and dates of English kings: William I, 1066, William II, 1087, Henry I, 1100. Meanwhile the fairy tales my mother read came from Andrew Lang or the Brothers Grimm – Grimm by name, grim by nature. We were wholly unfamiliar with the Children of Lir, Cuchulainn, Queen Maeve, Deidre of the Sorrows, or any of the other robust beings who dominated the Celtic tradition.

However, we knew that fairies existed – my father was familiar with the fairy shoe found in a field, three inches long, worn at the sole and heel, preserved in a tin box in Cousin Edith's house in West Cork. (It is still there.) Nanny Somers, believed in ghosts and terrified us with her stories when she was not washing for us, cooking for us, ironing our clothes and calling us Master.

She wore the conventional nursemaid's uniform, a white apron and buckled belt and thick serge stockings always on the point of slipping down. She had to climb the stairs to our lofty nursery far more times than the maids. In the nursery we tormented her, hiding her steel-framed spectacles and ignoring her plaintive cry of 'Boys, have you seen my glasses?' She tried to separate us when we fought. She would say occasionally, 'I'll tell your mother' – but she never did.

She sat and watched us play in the long garden behind the house, a rectangle curtained with high stone walls that offered few opportunities for games. At the far end was a coach house or mews turned into a garage where Dempsey the gardener lived. He did not have much gardening to do. Under the tall chestnut tree near my namesake's tombstone my father erected a swing. Nanny Somers could not prevent me falling off and breaking my arm. Phil pushed; on the highest point of the lift up I could see into neighbours' gardens, the same narrow rectangles, the same walls of foxy-coloured Georgian brick. Then a tumble and screams of agony, and Nanny in hysterics.

Later there was a smell of ether; I was in the Adelaide, my father's hospital, and he had set my arm. It was the only time that he doctored his children; Phil and I were always grateful that he did not imitate his colleague who one summer's afternoon put his three sons in deck chairs in their garden and took out all their tonsils. For a time I was a hero, rewarded with new toys and chocolate, my arm in a sling made from a silk scarf with black and orange stripes. Even today black and orange makes me think of pain.

I have a memory of walking beside the vast black double-hooded pram, with one hood up from which Phil peered out at the world. (We were so close in age that we took turns.) Before we emerged from the house for the afternoon walk we were dressed elaborately against the cold; the gaiters, with lines of buttons up our calves, took a long time to get fitted. 'Don't squirm, Master Peter.' Nanny's crinkled white head bent as she spent long minutes putting them in place with the steel button-hook.

Our destinations were dull. Often we only went a few steps away to the little private park in Fitzwilliam Square where other nannies gathered and knitted while we frolicked and fought. If the weather was good we would sometimes make the longer walk past the little kiosk in Leeson Street which sold newspapers, cigarettes and sweets; it is still there, a hazard to modern traffic, the word KIOSK written over it in capitals, one you don't come across much these days. We would make our way to Leeson Street Bridge and lean over to watch the barge horses, seen at a different angle from those viewed from the nursery.

'No throwing stones, Master Phil.'

With the rumbling sparking trams running beside us, we walked up to Herbert Park to feed the ducks on the lake. ('Don't step in that puddle, Master Peter.') We never went the other way towards York Street or the streets below Merrion Square where there was a sample of slums, although the most awful slums were north of the Liffey. Our lives were so circumscribed that we hardly ever saw a barefoot child. If we did, he would usually jeer at our strap shoes, buttoned-up coats, grey hats and gaiters.

2

Farmhill

M Y SECOND HOME was out in the suburbs south of
Dublin near Dundrum where we moved to live
with my grandfather. Farmhill was beside the little
village of Goatstown, which consisted of a line of cottages
and a ramshackle public house; these days The Goat has
become very smart. Three miles from Nelson's Pillar,
Farmhill's thirty-six acres, now covered with housing estates,
were then in the country. Within the high stone walls trees
lined the front and back avenues which were guarded by gate
lodges. Behind another high inner stone wall was the main
garden with glasshouses and long borders of flowers. The
woods and fields and the tennis court were typical of the
estates of the prosperous bourgeoisie lodged in their
comfortable houses on the outskirts of the city. The place
was run as a farm. We had our own sheep. cows, hens, geese,
pigs and vegetables. After the restrictions of Fitzwilliam
Place, Farmhill and its spaces were a boy's dream.

All round us were similar houses and estates. Just up the
lane was Campfield owned by the Pims who were Quakers,
and beyond, Airfield, where the Miss Overends lived behind
a huge cypress tree and a larger deodar; Airfield was also a
farm. Across the Harcourt Street Railway line the Shaw–
Smiths ran a nursery full of rare and exotic flowers on the

14

spacious acres of Ballawley. Not far from Goatstown was Newstead, belonging to my mother's family, which stood next door to Roebuck House, home to Maud Gonne MacBride and her wolfhounds and parrots and hangers-on. Before my mother met my father she had a crush on Maud Gonne's son, Sean, captivated by his skinny good looks, fruity French accent and the whiff of gunpowder about his reputation. It would not have been a liaison that met the approval of her family.

Farmhill was a big solid Victorian house with a hall running full length, full of animal heads and horns, and a number of huge reception rooms. Most of them had large plate glass windows and were north-facing, so they were cold for nine months of the year. There was central heating, but the huge coke furnace in the basement was seldom lighted, except on special occasions like Christmas Day. Central heating was considered effete and in any case it was not good for you; people said the two words in the tones of Edith Evans and the handbag. A friend of mine who lived in a very big house told me that she once fainted with the cold.

The vast billiard room with its cues and full-sized table was out of bounds. We had little inclination to go in there since even in midsummer it was chilly, although if you happened to be playing with ball and cue the exercise might have kept you warm. Uncle Bris and his brother, Uncle Phil, used to play, but no one went in there after Uncle Phil died, it was empty all the time.

We were also discouraged from going into the drawing room, although we used to sneak in to play the pianola. That was the sort of music I liked. Unlike Phil, I was totally unmusical – that particular fairy had not appeared at my christening. However, my parents refused to be discouraged and from an early age I was taught the piano and, worse, the recorder. Aunt Eileen made us pipes out of bamboo and tortured me with scales or forced me to renditions of 'Frère Jacques'. But I could joyfully play the pianola, the vulgar tasteless instrument, pumping the pedals, thumping out a Strauss waltz, or tunes from Gilbert and Sullivan. I could enjoy high speed and low speed and the clatter of the expired roll whirling around. Hidden under the piano seat were a dozen boxes with more compositions that we could effortlessly play until someone would hear and threaten to punish us.

The dining room was dominated by a huge sideboard weighed down with bosomy pieces of sterling silver, and lined with startling family portraits. We could study the neat beard of my grandfather above his clerical collar and the great uncles' white moustaches, large as sea birds. There were other portraits of plain people, long dead, including an early seventeenth-century Bishop of Cork so ugly that he was eventually given away. A bit of cheer came from the red and blue of the Turkey carpet.

Here my parents, my grandfather, Uncle Bris, when he was not staying with his mistress, and any guests that might be around, sat at a fat table covered with a shining linen cloth. On Sundays Phil and I were permitted to join the grown-ups; napkins tucked below our chins, we were given our own small table near the window. I remember eating chopped up roast beef with the help of a little silver hoe known as a pusher which children were issued with in those days. Before starting my grandfather would recite a long grace while the maids looked on. The grace would trigger the usual little air of unease that pervaded dining rooms where Catholic servants were employed by Protestants to wait on them. My wife says that this was more palpable in her grandparents' household when the diners got up and knelt beside their chairs to give thanks before their meals.

After grace we sat down to our meal, watched by the two maids in their black dresses, white caps with streamers and starched aprons. They stood by the sideboard, burdened with fat silver-plated tureens, like sentries listening to every word that was said. So conversation was fairly stilted. Occasionally someone might throw in a French phrase so that they should not understand – for example, mention of *le nez du Pape,* referring to the rear of a chicken.

My grandfather employed a housekeeper, Miss Moore, whose authority could never be questioned. No one could do anything in the house without her agreement. Bed-making, washing up in the pantry, picking fruit for jam, organising the day's vegetables to be carried in from the garden, storing apples, all that sort of thing was done under her direction. Fruit came from the walled garden, to be turned into more jam than the household could ever use. Boiling fruit and sugar were routinely pleasant odours coming from the kitchen at intervals throughout the year. Strawberry, raspberry, gooseberry and plum filtered through the house in summer, while every January oranges from Andalusia were bought in and thrown into cauldrons like tennis balls before being chopped up and converted to three hundred pots of marmalade, according to the housekeepers accounts – almost a pot for every day.

Naturally Miss Moore was responsible for meals. I have a housekeeper's book in which she planned our menus for

1937. The columns listed prices of the various items of food and people who ate the stuff, not only the adults and guests in the dining room, but the rest of the staff – 'Josie, Ann, May, Tracy and two men' and ourselves; except for Sundays, we were provided with our own separate portions in the nursery.

The cooking supervised by Miss Moore was not very good. Regularly the fresh produce gathered from the estate was boiled to pulp; a handful of bread soda was thrown in among the new peas to turn them emerald green. Spinach, for which we had the usual child's aversion also appeared in one of the brighter of the forty shades, and so did the Brussels sprouts, Miss Moore's favourite vegetable, while the pale subtle colour of the cabbage was suitably sea green, considering the water that came with it. In summer the lettuce appeared beside the cold ham and the slices of hard boiled egg without dressing. The warm sweet tomatoes from the greenhouses became cold and slimy. Beetroot in quantities made us pee puce.

Outside purchases from Findlater's and the butcher in Dundrum, carefully recorded in Miss Moore's book, were turned into rissoles, minced beef, minced turkey, cauliflower cheese, macaroni cheese, boiled bacon and cabbage, and braised liver. 'Corned Brisket 3s. 8d. 2 Ox-tails. 5½ pounds tail end 4s. 7d. 2 Rabbits no charge.' There were rabbits galore, eaten as a duty because they were so abundant, rabbit pie, rabbits in onion sauce and curried rabbits in order to disguise the taste. Currying, throwing a handful of curry powder and a few raisins into leftovers, was a favourite culinary tactic, and we ate plenty of curried mince and curried mutton. Boarding house desserts finished most meals

– steam pudding, milk pudding, marmalade pudding, rice pudding, semolina or jelly. And apple – stewed, Charlotte, baked with custard, or pie.

Occasionally the menu might been livened by birds shot by my Uncle Paddy. They were retrieved by Cicely, the springer spaniel named after a cousin who lived in Mayo. Her family was so poor that her brothers could not afford retrievers or hunting dogs, so Cousin Cicely used to put on her black bathing suit and plunge into the bog after the shot birds.

In those days game birds were still found in droves on the Dublin and Wicklow mountains. Zig-zagging snipe were hunted at the back of Ticknock, grouse around Djouce, and woodcock, sheltering in the Wicklow woods, having come in on the November full moon. Such birds were not for us. It was for the adults to tackle them as they lay on their slices of toast, little feet curled up; to crunch the marble sized skulls and pick out little brains with their forks.

In spring eggs appeared at meal after meal. In those days hens laid in the springtime, so that during March and April supper was dominated by fried eggs, poached eggs, scrambled eggs and, of course, curried eggs. There were plenty left over which were preserved in water-glass in zinc buckets from which they would emerge in winter, never quite fresh.

In early summer, when the mayfly were out, my uncles would send up trout caught in Lough Mask, wrapped in long grass which was supposed to keep them fresh. A little later the fishmongers sold the regular glut of salmon. Caught in dozens from every river in Ireland the huge noble fish, honoured by having their likeness engraved on every two-shilling piece, would appear hot or cold, served with bottled salad cream. I don't remember anyone really liking salmon and there were stories of servants going on strike if given too much of it. With or without salmon, every Friday the household had to brace itself for fish, steamed, smoked, fried or covered with white sauce. Although we did not know it at the time, eating fish of every variety turned out to be a good way of preparing us for our future life on our island.

Irish cooking generally had a poor reputation, though not every household went as far as our cousins in Meath who lived almost entirely out of hampers sent over from Harrods. But there were things to enjoy. The strawberries, ripened under nets, were succeeded by raspberries, also secured from birds in their cages, promoting the annual summer debate about which was the nicer. The cakes at teatime were delicious, the lemon sponges, the fruit cakes, the barm bracks at Halloween, and the heavy Christmas cake; we invariably had too much, and afterwards it felt as if we had been eating stones.

Sunday meals were sumptuous; as we returned from church at Taney and stepped into the hall of the house, the lines of stuffed animal heads on the walls seemed to be sniffing up the smell of roasting barons of beef and legs of lamb. After grace came the carving ceremony; my father might have been the surgeon, but it was my grandfather who made the fuss and flourish with the steel sharpener. Perhaps carving meat was a substitute for duelling? I remember Uncle Paddy's horror when he was old and saw the younger generation carving up meat with electric carving knives; the result was nothing like the slices of beef he used to distribute, thin as paper. The beef was never rare, no one liked that, it was always brown through and through. If my grandfather had been doing Shylock's work, he could probably have produced the pound of flesh without the drop of blood. It was a pity about the accompanying boiled carrots in corn-flour sauce and the chocolate brown gravy – the Bisto Kids were already at work.

For Phil and myself, all the acres of Farmhill were wonderful after our confined lives in Fitzwilliam Place. It was good to escape Nanny Somers and run around, climbing the largest possible trees and nearly falling, slamming croquet balls into shrubberies so that they were never found again, and generally making mischief.

The trees were full of crows and in spring when they were building they made an endless noise; even now, remembering that endless cawing, I find that the most beautiful birdsong is never the same. One year there was a gale and a good many fledglings were blown down to the ground, but not killed as they could just flutter. We collected them in a large wheel-barrow and brought them to the apple room in the yard where we kept them until they died one by one. They didn't die of starvation as we dug up worms for them. The Diet of Worms, as my grandfather called it, did them no good, poor creatures.

Farmhill might be in a Dublin suburb, but it had a strict old-fashioned country house layout. Following tradition and four hundred years of defensive architecture, the walled garden was kept at a distance from the house so that there was no impediment in the view, and croppies and rebels could be seen from the drawing room.

In the same way that Peter Rabbit and Benjamin Bunny sought to escape Mr MacGregor's attention, we avoided Rooney, the head gardener, who dug or saw that others dug, always dressed formally in a sombre dark blue suit, battered hat, laced up boots, buttoned-up shirt and a waistcoat, from which dangled the chain of his half-hunter. If he was in a good mood he would produce it for us.

'Blow it open, boys!'

Rooney with his waxy grey face ruled the garden as Miss Moore ruled the house. My mother tried to change this.

'I think, Rooney, that old climber should go. There's too much deadwood.'

'Yes, Ma'am.'

'Remember to put in celery when you are seeding the vegetables.'

'Yes, Ma'am.'

However often he touched his old grey bowler, they both knew that he took her orders as mere suggestions, and might or might not do what she asked. He did not like flowers at all. My grandfather once overheard him soliloquising: 'If there's one thing in this world I *hates* 'tis flowers. They're no use, nothing but a bother always.'

As well as the half-hunter, Rooney's waistcoat pocket had the keys to the glasshouses which were usually kept locked, especially in late summer as things grew ripe. But not always. Robbery was a matter of timing. An unlocked greenhouse meant fat peaches and grapes. There was the exhilaration of terror in the fact that he might catch us with a peach in a little fist.

'I'll get you . . . I have my eye on youse . . .' The eye was a startling blue, and it wandered as he grimaced alarmingly, clenching his bony knuckles.

'Do you think he'll kill us?'

In those days workmen and men blithely referred to as the

lower classes, lower orders, or even the natives (but that was a joke) were known only by their surnames, although their wives were given the honorific Mrs Rooney, Mrs Doyle. Rooney and his family lived in one lodge at the north end of the estate, Doyle, who looked after the farm, and his lot in the other to the south. Just for allowing those picturesque little dog kennels with no sanitation packed with children, the Anglo-Irish deserved to lose their power. At least Mrs Doyle and Mrs Rooney did not have to curtsy to the horse and carriage after they had opened the gates. There were still plenty of places in Ireland where that old custom continued.

Not long ago an American knocked on the door of my cousin's house outside Bray and asked if he could look at the gate lodge where his father, who had emigrated, had been brought up with six brothers and sisters. When we all went down and had a look at the little ruin, he couldn't believe it, and we were filled with shame. The gate lodges at Farmhill were no larger.

Rooney's rages were balanced by Doyle's 'small indispositions'. Doyle drank too much. Bribes and inducements were offered by my grandfather to persuade him to stop – packets of tea and a little more in the way of wages than the other men on the estate received. A week would go by, and just as my grandfather thought he was winning the battle for sobriety, Doyle would fall from grace again. Miss Moore, stern faced, would report: 'Canon, I saw him walking up the avenue swaying and singing.'

Once when Doyle was sent off like Beanstalk Jack to buy a cow, Miss Moore glimpsed him in the lower yard.

'Canon, he was milking the animal without a bucket and the milk was splashing all over the cobbles.'

This was a time when the bribes were stopped, but the much repeated anecdote made people laugh, and soon Doyle was receiving tea and half-crowns again.

While Rooney watched over his fruit and vegetables, and Doyle swayed after the cattle, my mother worked on the flowers. She had no other responsibility with regard to the running of the house, since Miss Moore ruled there. She did not mind at all. On most fine afternoons, accompanied by her dogs, she took her spade and with a look of rapture went down to the walled garden to dig. Colette saw the same look in her mother, Sido, and described it as her 'radiant garden face' (as opposed to the 'anxious indoor face'). Gardening was an obsession all the year round from the arrival of seed catalogues in the spring, to the fuzz of sprouting seedlings, and the cuttings with their curled white roots in the green-house to the glorious circus-coloured displays of summer.

In addition, my mother had the other preoccupations of Anglo-Irish ladies – animals and charities. Phil and I came much farther down her list of interests. One charity, linked to my father's profession, was associated with a children's surgical hospital located in Merrion Street. The terrible surgical conditions induced by TB were treated there with other horrors. One of Dublin's most expensive restaurants is now situated on the site of the hospital. I have eaten there once, and as I toyed with my one hundred pound meal, I could not help remembering the notice that used to be outside, proclaiming patients' problems – a list of brutal words like 'curvature of the spine, club feet, deformities'.

'Daddy cures those,' we used to say proudly if we were passing.

My mother collected money for this hospital, but her

main charitable work was associated with the Magdalen Asylum. This was located in a large rambling eighteenth-century house at the foot of Leeson Street. In the 1960s the building was an early victim to the destruction of Dublin's Georgian heritage, demolished to make room for a singularly ugly skyscraper, while the Asylum moved out to Donnybrook. For another couple of decades it continued to be dedicated to the purpose for which Lady Arabella Denny had founded it in the eighteenth century – providing a haven for fallen Protestant girls who were in the process of having babies.

Only first falls were accepted – second falls had to go to another, presumably less comfortable, refuge. My mother was on the Board that looked after the welfare of these superior Magdalens, who only recently had stopped wearing the eighteenth-century uniforms that Lady Denny had decreed. The Board also sought homes for the babies. It was easier to dispose of Protestant babies than Catholic because there were a lot fewer of them.

My mother devoted a good deal of time to the Magdalen Asylum and the ongoing problems of difficult or ungrateful girls, and the question that came up over and over again as to whether just this once a second fall might be admitted, but it was gardening that gave her the greatest joy. The dogs sat and watched as she dug, creating and encouraging the brilliant summer display of perennials in the long border. In autumn she saw to the spread of bulbs; when Harold Nicolson visited Farmhill during the Emergency after the place had been turned into the British Residency, he noticed my mother's snowdrops and mentioned them in his diary. Regularly Rooney would send in one of his boys with a large basket of flowers to decorate the various rooms. My mother had her flower room with a sink filled with vases and, after each one was filled, a maid would carry it to the designated room, even the unused billiard room.

No one took much notice of us, although Nanny Somers came outside regularly and called plaintively. By this time we rode bicycles which we had received at our first Christmas at Farmhill. The house had been greatly cheered up by the huge amounts of holly and ivy brought in by Rooney and his men, together with the Christmas tree that reached well up to the height of the heads of *ovis poli* and sambur shot and stuffed by Uncle Phil. Relatives I had never seen before suddenly appeared to be treated to slivers from the ostrich-sized turkey. We had some decent presents from Father Christmas, having borrowed my father's most ample socks. (He had huge feet which were known as the *Mauritania* and the *Aquitania*.) But best of all that day was finding our bikes hidden behind the drawing room curtains.

The back avenue leading down from the Doyles' lodge proved an ideal testing ground, and here we raced up and down while Nanny Somers flapped and clucked like a hen seeing the ducklings she had brought up go into the water. It was soon after receiving our first bikes that she vanished.

Today when I meet certain aging contemporaries we discuss Nanny Somers, who was handed from one family to another like a baton in a relay race. However monstrously we had behaved to her, she always made out to each set of children that the last ones she had worked for were saintly perfection.

The two large yards behind the main house were good places for games and explorations. In the lower yard were the dairy and the laundry room. No need at Farmhill for deliveries from the Swastika Laundry. On wash days Mrs Doyle stood among the tubs of boiling water fighting the week's washing with washboard and red Sunlight soap and starch and soda before ironing with numerous flat irons kept heating on a large stove.

Besides our shirts and socks, all the household linen went into the tubs, including the white damask tablecloths with their figured flowered satin patterns and the napkins that lasted us a week, a little dirtier each time they were curled up in our silver napkin rings. Handkerchiefs lost their snot in the face of clouds of steam and Mrs Doyle's vigorous rubbing on the glass-fronted scrubbing board.

In later years my mother would cling to the vestiges of old decency with the aid of her new washing machine. She adhered to those linen napkins and handkerchiefs, since paper napkins and Kleenex, like lined writing paper and fish knives, remained unforgivably vulgar.

Very soon after we arrived in Farmhill we discovered the most wonderful toy in the lower yard. One summer day, having evaded Nanny Somers, we were exploring the area beyond the steaming laundry room. There was a line of sheds where hooks for harness remained and a little room for the coachman. No coachman or chauffeur now, the adults drove their own. Beside their cars which were parked in various stables, was also a strange room kept closed, but not locked or bolted.

'What's in here?' We pushed a creaking door, and went into a dark place, with a smell of of old hay, where there was parked an ancient car, old even for the 1930s. We could make out great nickel-plated headlamps and gigantic wheels.

'Climb up!'

Phil was the older and stronger and clambered up more easily, so he got to the driver's seat first. Our legs dangled over the high musty-smelling leather seats, modelled on a king's carriage, as he seized the small wooden steering wheel and pumped the brass plungers that decorated the dashboard. I tackled the horn and a blast filled the shed.

'Shut up! Someone will hear!'

Without a word we knew that this was our secret. Meanwhile, what if the venerable vehicle broke into life, and we could go with it like Mr Toad out of its prison and out onto the empty country roads of south Dublin?

For most of that summer this dark shed was our favourite place of play, and every time we shook off the grown-ups and made our way into our hiding place, we took the strange old car for imaginary drives.

Inevitably we played too long, for the time came when Nanny Somers managed to track us down, peering round the half-closed door of the shed, her cries bordering on hysteria.

'Get down, get down, get out of there! – You'll have me murdered!' And although we went on playing there, some of the joy had gone out of it – from now on she knew where to find us.

The car in which we played was no ordinary vehicle. It was the Silver Stream.

The Silver Stream five-seater *Roi des Belges* Touring Car was the brainchild of our Great Uncle Phil who had been a railway engineer, and had built swathes of railway lines in India and organised others in China. He also advised some rajahs about their own private railways. He retired at a relatively early age because of his health, rich and successful, very much the nabob. He bought a house in Carnalway, County Kildare, where my grandfather was rector and found he had time on his hands.

In the early years of the twentieth century he became dissatisfied with the car he owned, a four-cylinder De Dietrich, and having decided that in fact all motor cars of the period were unreliable, determined to build a car that would surpass the rest. It would be an improvement on Royce's Silver Ghost. In 1906, he and Uncle Bris, who had also made a lot of money, formed a company and set about designing a unique vehicle, consulting motoring journals and catalogues of car parts.

Uncle Phil selected a rolling chassis from a French motor agents, Malicet et Blin, and a six-cylinder engine from Gnome et Rhône, a firm which later was among the first to manufacture rotary aero engines. From British, French and Belgian catalogues he accumulated the most expensive automobile parts which he assembled into a car with an elaborate open touring body that was first driven proudly on the dusty roads of Kildare around 1908. But for whatever reason, it was not taken out very much, and by the time it ended up in the shed in Farmhill there was little mileage on its clock.

Where did the name come from? Perhaps Uncle Phil thought up the name Silver Stream after reading Tennyson's *The Brook* – 'For men may come and men may go, but I go on for ever' – an excellent sentiment for any business. Or he may have been inspired by the River Liffey that ran by Carnalway Rectory. Or perhaps the name was in direct rivalry to Silver Ghost. The prototype Silver Stream cost twice as much as the car put together by Mr Rolls and Mr

Royce – two thousand pounds, enough to buy a decent town house. This was probably the reason that Uncle Phil's and Uncle Bris's motor company never prospered and only one car of its kind was ever built.

Uncle Phil was proud of his creation. He considered that the Royal Irish Automobile Club should recognise his achievement and designed a crest for them incorporating the device that appeared on the silver forks with which we ate Miss Moore's braised steak and cottage pie. Derived from the Somerville family crest, it consisted of 'a dragon . . . charged with a trefoil, or spouting out fire, behind and before, standing on a wheel'.

Uncle Phil was aware that a thousand years ago a Somerville knight was called upon to kill a 'warrum' – a fearsome fiery dragon who lived in a field in the Scottish borders. The knight was evidently an engineer, like Uncle Phil, since he designed a weapon consisting of a spear attached to a wheel and, with his servant, approached the creature.

We liked the story better than the usual fairy tale.

About the sun rysing, this serpent or worme . . . appeared with her head and some part of her body without the den. Whereupon the servant . . . set fyre to the peats upon the wheel of the lance, and instantly this resolute gentleman put spurs to his horse, advanced with full gallop, the fyre still increasing, placed the same with the wheel and almost the third part of his lance, directly into the serpent's mouth, which went doune her throat into her bellie, which he left there . . . giving her a deadly wound.

Alas, the RIAC rejected Uncle Phil's design and chose a more prosaic one of their own.

The Silver Stream stayed in the family for another forty years. In the late seventies the grand old car, the worse for wear after we had played with it and the mice and moth and dust had got to it, was put up for sale for two thousand pounds. The enthusiast who came to buy it almost killed himself with the speed he drove to get there first. He did it up, with the fanaticism that such people show, and it became famous. Ireland's unique contribution to motoring history, has appeared on stamps, banknotes and inevitably on table mats where it is shown carrying a lady passenger in a long dress, wearing a veil. We have been told often enough that it is now priceless. At least Phil and I got some fun out of it.

The Silver Stream was not the only unusual car in the neighbourhood of Dundrum. Our neighbours were Miss Laetitia and Miss Naomi Overend who lived nearby at Airfield. Their farm had a herd of Jersey cows that regularly won rosettes at the Spring Show. Tinkerbelle, the most interesting cow, was eighteen years old – no one had had the heart to slaughter her or get rid of her, and she continued into her twenties, her skin in folds like a bloodhound, her thigh bones sticking out behind her melancholy face like an extra pair of horns.

Naomi was my godmother. She was the best possible – not a birthday or Christmas went by without a substantial present. There was the year of the toy trumpet, the year of the Hiawatha suit and later the years of the five pound note. Naomi's elder sister, Miss Laetitia, known as Tot by a very few favoured people, had an air of queenly authority, and was a Dame of St John's Ambulance.

Although the sisters were extremely rich – even richer than we were – they lived austerely. They wore practical mannish clothes, noted down all their expenses, such as cups of coffee at the Country Shop or lunch at the Royal Irish Automobile Club in Dawson Street, in little notebooks, and their house was freezing, colder even than Farmhill. But they had one great extravagance and that was their cars.

Naomi's was the more modest as befitted a younger sister – an Austin Tourer with its specially built Tickford cabriolet touring body which was bought in 1936 for £688. 6s. 7½d. Tot's car had been acquired a decade earlier, a Roll-Royce 20 Open Tourer, old enough to carry the red RR badge.

Tot and Naomi maintained their cars from the moment of purchase; no lesser mortals or mechanics could be trusted to do the work. It was fascinating to see Tot, grimly familiar in her tailored suit with the squared shoulders, after she had changed into a pair of overalls and trousers; we were allowed to watch as she stretched flat, her legs sticking out from under the Rolls, performing some essential service with an oil can.

The Miss Overends' Rolls and Austin had one great advantage over the Silver Stream – they were still on the road. Going for a drive with either Tot or Naomi in one or other of their regal dark blue cars was all very well, but later with the increase of traffic became an ordeal. Tot and Naomi had a similar style of driving, proceeding at a steady thirty miles an hour on the crown of the road, oblivious of honks and beeps from other motorists. With a break for the Emergency, both cars continued to be driven up until the 1960s.

The sisters bequeathed Airfield to the people of Dublin,

over thirty acres of fields lying among cluttered suburbs. The cars are there in a special garage. The gardens and the farm with cows sheep and hens are all preserved and when I walk through Murray's field and Tot's garden and inspect the Overends' pet cemetery, I feel I am back in the Dundrum of the 1930s.

We never remembered Uncle Phil, but Uncle Bris was still a strong, terrifying presence. He lived half the time at Farmhill, with his brother, my grandfather, and half the time with Miss Widdy. His wife, Allie, was lodged in a substantial house called Ardmore which is now part of University College, Dublin. He and Allie had separated many years before. We were told that he had abandoned her penniless in Malta and his regiment had a whip around to enable her to get back to Ireland.

Like so many country houses, Farmhill was full of souvenirs brought back from the east, an eclectic medley of things beautiful and hideous. They were mostly hideous, except for the things from China, the *famille rose* tureens and plates that had come to Ireland, together with crates of tea, during the eighteenth century, and the curtains decorated with cranes and flowers, said to have been acquired after the sack of Peking. A lot of families with imperial connections had loot from Peking – nothing to be proud of.

Uncle Phil's contribution to country house decor was conventional – a variety of butchered and beheaded animals, which must have taken him years of stalking the Himalayas to accumulate. Like other old Indian hands he was also responsible for the Benares brass, and the ebony and ivory elephants. Was there nothing else to buy in India?

But it was Uncle Bris's taste that dominated Farmhill.

Everywhere were huge Majolica jars, enough to accommodate the forty thieves, covered with crowns, crests, swords and depictions of knights and ladies. He had discovered them in a cellar of a building associated with the Knights of Malta. Did he help himself, did he buy them, or were they given to him by some grateful Maltese? We could only guess.

Later we coined a word 'Brisbania' to describe the jars, the Satsuma china, the profusely decorated oriental tea cabinets, stands, ebony tables, and ornately carved chairs that no one could sit on, and the bronze gong in the hall that summoned us to our meals, supported by a huge snarling ebony dragon not unlike the one that curled around Uncle Bris's back.

The twirly black cabinet in the drawing room displayed a number of fine ivory carvings of torture scenes. There was a little man three inches high being sawn in two, an exquisitely rendered decapitated corpse, lacquer blood flowing from his neck and a prisoner being squeezed to death in an ingenious wooden grip. From time to time on rainy days Phil and I played with them, a change from Meccano and lead soldiers.

Uncle Bris had acquired the furniture and torture scenes in Japan, which he visited around 1880. He got his tattoos there as well. He had a photograph taken of himself in the days when he was young and his Dundreary moustache was brown, proudly showing a selection of them. He is wearing a vest which is drawn back to reveal the butterfly and dragon flying above his nipples. We were told that the walking reptile house, which was Uncle Bris, was linked to a Japanese secret society and every member had to have the same sort of wriggling things stretched over their skins.

An album of pleasing photographs of Japanese scenes from this period includes some Japanese ladies standing around a

wooden tub. Perhaps it was fanciful to assume that the prim
little lady wearing a bun waiting her turn for a bath in a
wooden tub had a resemblance to his mistress. Miss Widdy
was so respectable that when we were a little older we were
regularly taken to have tea with her in her dour house in
Pembroke Road. In the drawing room where a black ebony
clock chimed from time to time, we were given slices of
barm brack arranged on a cake stand with silver plates
designed like lotus leaves. The room contained several pieces
of oriental furniture similar to those which cluttered up
Farmhill. There was also a large Bible prominently displayed.

Miss Widdy was a disappointment to sophisticated boys
like ourselves who expected a scarlet woman.

'She doesn't wear lipstick! She doesn't even smoke!'

After Uncle Bris had gone to live more or less permanently in Pembroke Road, it was decreed that some
members of the family had to stay on in Farmhill with my
grandfather, the Canon. It was thought unsuitable for Miss
Moore and my grandfather, who by the mid-1930s was
approaching his ninetieth year, to be cohabiting. The Canon,
was, after all, a clergyman. Probably because of the opportunities for gardening my mother was content at Farmhill.

Uncle Bris turned up regularly at Farmhill – never with
Miss Widdy – laughing heartily, and teasing us, although only
the smashed Easter egg remains in my mind. He was long
retired after a career as an army surgeon, mainly in the Far
East – the Straits Settlements, Singapore, Penang and Perak.
In Singapore, besides his military duties, he had a good
private practice, and found that the Chinese merchants paid
him well for his services. During the time he spent in the
East his chief hobby was orchids.

In those days a lot of money could be made out of orchids. Propagation was not easy nor speedy until the development of the meristem system, but the demand was great. At the turn of the century one English orchid-grower had a stock worth over ten thousand pounds. Like the diamond, the rare and beautiful tropical orchid was a status symbol. Uncle Bris's collection was huge and when he returned to Europe he sold it at an immense profit.

Later he served as a field surgeon in the Boer War. The photographs he took of tents full of wounded beside dusty South African battlefields and the box of surgical instruments that he used to saw off arms and legs on the battlefield are now in a medical museum. Many years later I met an old soldier who as a young officer was detailed to accompany Uncle Bris over the veld. By now a grizzled colonel, he had not forgotten how much he disliked the bossy surgeon with the white moustache. He told us: 'Ghastly man, Brisbane. At least I was able to blackball him for the Kildare Street Club!' There was another story of Uncle Bris insisting on driving a visiting general around the Curragh in pouring rain; the general died of pneumonia.

When he retired from the army Uncle Bris found another occupation, or perhaps hobby, which he continued to pursue to the end of his days – a long love affair with the stock exchange. He spent his days in speculation, studying his stocks and shares and buying with a flair that never deserted him. Besides tickets to Royal Dublin Society recitals, his fellow's ticket to the Royal Geographical Society (they accepted him, even if the Kildare Street Club did not), times of trams and tides, and his visiting cards, his wallet was always full of newspaper cuttings concerning prospectuses and information on new issues and promised dividends.

> Speculative Attractions of Brazilian Loans . . . This evidence that the State of San Paulo will pay if funds permit is a bull point for Brazilian Government bonds, and undoubtedly many of these look cheap . . .

His investments included Anglo-Persian Oil, Royal Dutch Petroleum, Arthur Guinness, Egyptian Delta Light Rail, Canadian General Electric, Canadian Pacific Railway, Great Northern Rail, USA War Loan, Belgium Loan, International Nickel Co. of Canada, the Kelvin Jute Company, Rand Mines Ltd, Italian Credit Consortium, Colombian Republic 5 per cent, New Zealand Government 4½ per cent, Northern France Railway, Colombian Republic 6 per cent, Orleans Railway 6 per cent and Johnson, Mooney and O'Brien.

And many more – Monterey Rail Light and Power Co., The Great Southern Railway, Rumanian 4 per cent, City of Saarbrucken 6 per cent, Tokyo 5½ per cent, City of Berlin 6 per cent, Greek 6 per cent, Stabilisation Loan. He weathered the crash of 1929, since there is no indication of even a tremor affecting his lifestyle and our own at Farmhill.

Both Uncle Bris and Uncle Phil were childless. They could indulge in their dream of setting up a motor company to rival Rolls-Royce. Later, through their generosity, my father and his brothers benefited, and my father was able to indulge his dream of creating an island kingdom.

3

My Grandfather

MY GRANDFATHER regularly ventured out to enjoy the garden and the latest array of flowers my mother had encouraged to bloom. At other times he would walk around the estate or be driven out to Dundrum by Miss Moore in his small Austin.

Most days someone would walk up the long winding avenue looking for charity and they rarely left without some help from him. There were the regulars like old Billy with the rheumy eyes and the clothes which smelt of everything – manure, horse, tobacco, mixed with the sour smell you got when you boarded a bus. (But we never did.) 'It's a terrible dirty old world!' he once said to us. Billy would sit outside the kitchen with a mug of tea and a slice of bread which he mumbled in his toothless jaw, telling us improbable stories which always ended with 'and that's the honest truth!'

Another person who called from time to time was Rose, wearing her feathered hat and walking straight into any room saying, 'Bless all here!' before falling on her knees.

'In Rose,' my grandfather would say, 'the Holy Spirit works its own particular grace.'

His study had escaped the touch of Uncle Bris and was furnished with conventional clergy taste. The pitch pine book cases contained hundreds of holy books – collections of sermons, discourses on Church of Ireland doctrine, commentaries on passages of the Bible and biographies of St Paul, Moses, and other great figures of the Old and New Testaments. On one wall was the 'Light of The World' that universal Protestant icon; like many Victorian Christians, my grandfather found the symbolism an important aid to his faith.

Once he pointed out to us how the weed-covered doors of our hard little hearts, shut and locked from within, awaited the knock of the crowned figure with the shining eyes lit by moonlight and lamplight whom I found altogether too ghostly for comfort. That was the occasion of the conkers. Near the front gate were chestnut trees and one September we collected conkers to throw at passing traffic. Not many vehicles trundled down towards Goatstown, so we aimed all our missiles at the Leveret and Fry van that turned in to deliver groceries to the house. The irate driver had us brought to Grandfather. It was like making rain in Fitzwilliam Place all over again and, although he did not beat us, he gave us a terrific scolding. I remember his dark brown eyes and the curious smell of his long white beard, like hay – a lot more pleasant than that which came from Billy.

Very subdued, we went to my mother for comfort. She wasn't much help. 'Grandad believes not only in a God of love but a God of anger. Don't throw stones or conkers again.'

The aura of piety at Farmhill sent me looking for God who, I had been told, was everywhere. 'Hello, God,' I addressed a visiting archdeacon, looking up at a tall man in an old-fashioned clerical hat and buttoned gaiters like those I wore myself. I despaired of finding Him, after a thorough search that mightily amused the grown-ups. But perhaps my hunt, which took me to the the greenhouses, the mouldy straw behind the

Silver Stream, and finally had me looking down the lavatory, was just as logical as my grandfather's communications with my dead grandmother which came about from his regular practice of spiritualism.

His memories of long years working for the Church of Ireland were vivid. Inevitably his fervently held belief in the truth of the Protestant faith resulted in forms of prejudice. He had the obsession about mixed marriages which was so common in Ireland at that time. If someone married a Catholic, a 'Roman Catholic', it was a tragedy as if he had drowned.

At Carnalway in County Kildare, where he had been rector for many years, the family had enjoyed a mysterious running joke about the cockatoo. 'Poor Cocky can't go to church, poor Cocky is a Roman Catholic.' (Cocky was brought to Farmhill, but to our regret he died before we came to live there. My grandfather used to point out to us the hollow tree on the avenue where he used to roost when he was not confined to his cage and the sound of his jabbering stifled by a green baize cloth.)

The Canon wrote frequently about what he called 'RC difficulties' including anecdotes about snatching dying people from priests and returning them to the true Protestant faith. But although he was not above proselytising, he could record a story against himself.

'Have you ever thought, Denis, to consider how much more prosperous in peace and successful in war are law-abiding Protestant nations than Roman Catholic ones?'

'Yes, your Reverence. You have your portion in this life.'

Every day he sat writing at his roll-top desk. He had retired from active ministry, having reached the rank, if that is what you call it, of Canon. So he no longer had to compose sermons, but he wrote regular letters to the *Irish Times*. He preserved them, and had reason to be proud of one, written at the end of October 1920, protesting at the barbarity of hanging a boy of eighteen. It was published the day before Kevin Barry's execution.

He condemned

> the politically stupid and morally iniquitous treatment of captured 'Republican soldiers' . . . The conscience of nine-tenths of the Irish Celtic nation – one of the most sincerely religious of nations – protests against these men being dealt with as common murderers, and maintains that they should be regarded as prisoners of war, and not confined in common prisons, sentenced to hard labour – still less, shot or hanged – unless when proved to have been spies or murderers of unarmed civilians or users of dum-dum bullets . . .

Years later when Ireland had gained her independence he wrote:

> as to the political situation, I maintained then, as I do now, that foolish Ireland was sufficiently grown-up to claim separation from England, if she really desired it.

When he was not corresponding with the *Irish Times*, he was writing his reminiscences which included his extensive family history. He did this for many years, and they contain copious anecdotes about forgotten people.

'The Venerable Zachary Cooke-Collis was vulgarly known as the

'Hot Gospeller'. He had a brother John who never married and was vulgarly known as 'The Boy who clung to the Rock', which he had done for three days at the shipwreck of the ill-fated *Killarney*, one of the first steam-ships to attempt a voyage to America. He was the only one saved . . .

I learn that the original Brisbane Warren, named after the Governor of New South Wales, whose name I bear, was 'even with his wife's fortune, but a poor country gentleman of extravagant taste'. I take after him.

I am intrigued to read of my Morgan relatives who had seventeen children, many of whom were unfortunate.

Ann was drowned after falling into an ornamental pond. Elizabeth was burned to death while threading a needle, the end of which she burned in a candle. Eliza died from rupture of a blood-vessel while dancing. Another girl from taking an overdose of bella donna before a dance (which she had heard would give lustre to her eyes). No sooner had she begun to dance, than she began to fall asleep. They hurriedly sent for a doctor who said that if she went to sleep she would die, so the family and guests spent the night in dragging her up and down stairs, but all to no purpose. Nothing could wake her, she died at 2 in the morning. Roland went to sea, and was never heard of again. Isaac fell into the river while crossing the gang-board into the ship, which broke his ribs and caused his death. Others died, also from accidents.

My grandfather was brought up in Cork and his people came from there or from the hallowed ground stretching from the west of the city to Mizen Head and Bantry. Like most of his relatives, he believed that this scattered tribe was infinitely superior to any other. This was in spite of the drunkards, eccentrics and madmen that appeared regularly in the forest of family trees.

> We were brought up to think that no one else in the world was as nice as our own kith and kin, and as they easily numbered one hundred, we had plenty to choose from.

Cousin Edith Somerville shared the view that this blend of planters, Cromwellians, Huguenots and such like, located in West Cork was special. 'There is something undoubtedly gratifying to the family that it should be spoken of as a "race" – a people apart,' she wrote in her inevitable family history.

In the drawing room of Farmhill arranged around the fireplace were numerous miniatures painted by the Cork miniaturist, Frederick Buck. These stiff pink-cheeked militia men, gentlemen in throttling white cravats and young women in white décolleté, invariably painted in three-quarter face, looking to the right, were a positive proof of our Cork ancestry. For a span of thirty years from about 1785 to at least 1815 anyone in Cork who had social pretensions had themselves painted by Buck, whose output is the reason why county families who hail from Cork have more miniatures than anyone else in Ireland.

My grandfather wrote how

> my early memories are all connected with the City and County of Cork. And in my old age my heart goes back with affection to the beauty of this the most Southern County in Ireland, and I love the people with all their provincialisms in thought and

speech, their courtesies and camaraderie and pleasing conviction of their own superiority.

Here he is writing about Corkonians both Catholic and Protestant, who to this day continue to be complacent about their virtues. But the emphasis of his recollections is on the superiority of his own cousins and connections, however unsatisfactory individuals might be.

She also was a Somerville, a daughter of my mother's eldest brother Thomas . . . The less asked about his descendants the better. The result of too much inbreeding is not good for man or beast . . .

Mr De Burgh of Kilfinane Castle, a dirty, hard-drinking but scholarly old man, whose wife was one of the Townsends of Shepperton, and whose pretty daughter . . . Jane de Burgh, married first of all 'Mr Glory' Townsend of the Castle, and after his death from drink, married a Mr Cave . . .

Other relatives and connections became rakes or spend-thrifts and my grandfather doggedly recorded their fate. There was the cousin who 'in the end, heavily in debt, cheated his creditors by disappearing one night from the deck of the Holyhead to Kingston mail boat'. Another came from

a very Godless family . . . It was his proud boast that a hundred wax candles were burnt in the house every night, and as there was a large cut glass chandelier in the hall and others in the dining room and drawing room fitted with candles, and all three lighted every night, it was probably true, so no wonder the family is now poor.

44

There was the Townsend of Whitehall whose

drunken fury blazed forth against the portraits of his ancestors and he used to get his revolver and fire at them . . . He finally died of drink. The portraits, full of holes, were then taken down and sent away to be repaired and came back beautifully done and just like new.

My grandfather's reminiscences read feebly in comparison to those of his own grandfather, William Large, who flourished at the end of the eighteenth and the beginning of the nineteenth centuries. Like many other Cork merchants, William Large was involved in the sugar trade, setting out as a young man from Cork to work with his uncle who had a plantation in Barbados.

He attended slave auctions fortified by 'sangrena' (Madeira and hot water). He describes a young woman at Port Royal bought by a Royal Naval officer and set free to 'the hearty cheering of the people'. He recorded some terrible incidents dispassionately.

I saw a fine stately black woman with a child in her arms crossing a bridge under which ran a deep stream of water followed by two Negro drivers, flogging her with the greatest violence. The child was struck and screamed, when the poor creature in frenzy, dashed it over the bridge, and jumped after it, but a boat being at hand, she was saved, brought on shore and received thirty-one lashes.

William Large acquired slaves of his own. Among his possessions was Dublin, 'a most faithful creature', and Old

Jeffrey, whom he inherited from his uncle. 'Loyal' though Old Jeffrey might be, he openly resented his slavery. He had a pet monkey which he believed contained the soul of the captain who had stolen him from Africa.

> Every day he used to tie up the monkey to give him so many lashes; while the poor animal was screaming he would invariably call out: 'Sh, Captain, that's for the bad treatment you gave me long ago.'

In due course William Large retired from Barbados. He came back to Cork in a brig captured by the French, which he had acquired for two thousand pounds. The *Generous Friend* was refitted and sent to Surinam with a full cargo of Irish goods;

> she made a most successful voyage, and returned with a full cargo of sugars, which realised a profit of £800 ... after this I established myself fully as a merchant in my native city in the year 1810.

He does not relate in his memoir how he brought back from the West Indies two of his children who had a black mother. Nor is there evidence about her or her fate, or even whether she was alive when her son and daughter came to Cork together with their father.

There was no attempt to conceal the existence of these children, and my own grandfather wrote cheerfully about his half-aunt and uncle. They were properly educated and given the conventional upbringing of the day. The boy, also named William, trained as a doctor. Recently I received a letter from

Dr Hart of the University of Ulster, who is making a study of black people in Ireland.

> There is a record of a William Large, born in the West Indies, having become a student at Trinity College on May 3rd, 1824. He was the son of William Large, a merchant. What particularly intrigues me about him is that there was a story which appeared in instalments of the *Illustrated Dublin Journal* in 1861–62 called 'The Black Doctor'. The hero is a black man of West Indian origin with a medical training moving in Dublin's underworld in the early years of the century, who saves some respectable middle-class Irish people from the clutches of a money-lender, but dies of a broken heart . . . when the sister of one of those saved rejects him on account of his colour.

In my grandfather's reminiscences he writes of how William Large, his half-uncle became the companion of

> ruined gamblers and night walkers of high and low degree . . . he was so wild and extravagant that my grandfather at length allowed him to taste the sweets of a debtor's prison before paying his debts and sending him and his wife to Australia.

It seems very possible that the author of 'The Black Doctor' obtained the idea of his lurid melodrama from the situation of William Large. Perhaps the author was letting his imagination run riot when he depicted the Black Doctor as

> below the middle height, and stout, approaching to corpulency. His dark hair, sooty black, crisped into small black curls over a large head that seemed too heavy for the stout little man who

had to carry it. His forehead was low, though broad and massive, and his nose was elevated above a heavy sensual mouth, armed with large teeth, that looked entirely white, because of the contrast which they formed to the dark hue of his face.

Old William Large settled down with a second family. One of his sons, Richard, my great-grandfather, married Elizabeth Somerville, a tough lady who was reluctant to relinquish her maiden name. So a top-heavy double-barrelled combination came into being and we became Somerville-Larges.

Richard Somerville-Large's eldest son, William, my grandfather, was born at one of the darkest moments in Ireland's history, in December 1847. A cousin remembered how

we saw black spots on the leaves of the potato fields; and in most cases this steadily increased, and the smell everywhere became sickening. When dug the roots were black, and could not be eaten. People cut off the stalks with a scythe, thinking that could save them. The spray was unknown then.

For my grandfather's relatives it was a world of soup kitchens that every household maintained. Later a number of them wrote down their memories, recording moments of horror:

Just outside the gate I saw a poor woman sitting on the foot-path, surrounded by her starving children. I at once ran back to the house, where we always had soup ready, and brought back a jug of food and tin cans. The poor woman was dead when I returned. I laid her on the footpath, fed the poor little children, and sent them in the cart to the Poor House.

. . . Another day, coming home to luncheon, I saw a poor man trying to get a seat in the wheelbarrow where our men were cleaning the gravel. He looked very bad, and I hastened to the house for food. He was dead in the wheelbarrow when I got back.

Households were cut down:

We gave up two horses, retaining one and a donkey. Dogs were also killed, and many persons gave up having wine or any stimulant. Our teachers, governesses, butler and other dependents were parted with, and the house was reduced to a very low ebb in every way.

Like Noah and his family, safe in their Ark, surrounded by thousands who were being swept to destruction, it seemed by God's command, few of these people would perish, although some would die of fever. They could always be 'coming home to luncheon'. No one would actually starve.

After the famine ceased to be a daily horror, many whose livelihood came from the pernicious agricultural system that depended on rents became much poorer. Often the onset of relative poverty was gradual and decades would pass before the old elegant lifestyle in the big house had to be abandoned.

My grandfather was a firm believer in ghosts, like the one he encountered as a boy in a house in a remote part of West Cork, where ghostly footsteps were often heard. One night a housemaid was heard shrieking on the stairs. 'Oh, Father Tom, if it's you, for God's sake speak to me.' Father Tom was a young priest, engaged as a tutor to Cousin John's children, and the apparition was outside his bedroom door. When he opened it he immediately slammed it, and could never be induced to say what he had seen. The old cook, however, soothed the housemaid, 'Sure it's only the old Colonel, he won't do you a bit of harm.'

Ghosts, vacant white faces and sounds of chains were part of the furnishings of lonely houses lit with colza lamps and wax candles. They frequented the Dublin suburbs. A ghost was supposed to linger near the tennis court at Farmhill, perhaps seeking a partner to play with. The idea of him terrified me.

At the same time gloomy interiors and confident belief in the hereafter encouraged spiritualism. One of my grandfather's many cousins was a founder member of the Society for Psychical Research, and with the help of the medium, Daniel Dunglass Home, once levitated in his chair and wrote his name on the ceiling. A regular visitor to many big houses was the medium, adept at controlling table tapping, Ouija boards and spirit writing, often an intelligent spinster lady, to act as a link with the dead.

Cousin Edith was a dogged practitioner of spiritualism. Every day the dead communicated with her in writing which went on and on, with the words all joined up, and had to be deciphered afterwards. When Edith's brother, Boyle Somerville, was shot on the doorstep of his house, Drishane, he was soon summoned by his sister for a chat, with little time to settle into the next life.

Cousin Edith wrote many of her books with aid from the departed, not only Violet Martin, her collaborator in life, but a number of her forebears. When compiling a family history, could anything be more convenient that consulting an ancestor to confirm details? Who better to summon up than the Reverend Thomas Somerville who had died in 1740? 'I am, my dear descendant, the first of our line to hold this living,' he wrote, using the squiggly lettering that had to be interpreted by a medium. 'I am preparing to instruct you – I was the second cousin of my Lord Somerville . . .'

The Reverend Thomas described to Edith his parish in Castlehaven in West Cork at the beginning of the eighteenth century where he lived comfortably in the old O'Driscoll castle.

> There were some two hundred yeomen and gentlefolk . . . They were zealous worshippers and pretty compliments were paid me for my sermons . . . Ireland was a savage and barbarous country. We did not communicate save when necessary with the common Irish . . . I spoke to them through an interpreter, but I obtained some proficiency in the tongue in my old age. I sorrowed because of their being in the darkness and unacquainted with the true faith.

In the hereafter my grandfather would have the company of two wives, and meanwhile he regularly got in contact with both of them, exchanging laughter and jokes as they waited for him on the other side. After his death a suitcase of his was found filled with pages of spirit writing.

I never heard if he tried to get in touch with his father, Richard Large, who died when he was sixteen. ('First crutches, then the bath-chair stage, and finally for some years seldom out of bed.') However distressing his father's long illness which haunted his boyhood, the Canon's religious belief was unshaken and later strengthened. 'When in the Divinity

School I contracted a strong conviction of the unanswerable strength of the Protestant position.' He became a clergyman, one of the last to be ordained before the disestablishment of the Church of Ireland in 1869.

His first wife, a Miss Maunsell, died in childbirth; the baby who survived became my Aunt Alice. Ten years later he married my grandmother, Bessie Fleming, another distant cousin who lived in West Cork in a house called New Court outside Skibbereen.

My Uncle Becher once met an old woman who remembered New Court in the days of its glory and sang to him a poem composed by her brother.

Oh New Court is the prettiest place in Carbery I ween,
Environed by great grandeur, and pine-groves ever green,
It also is an ancient place of fame and high renown
Prettily situated and convenient to the town.

Where the sportsman with his fowling-piece the gay domain
    traversed,
And the gentry of Rosscarbery met, and lingered and conversed,
They joined in festive splendour and enjoyed it with great zest
And they sang the praise of New Court, for it always was the
    best.

My grandmother, born Bessie Fleming, known to her family as Sunshine, grew up at New Court with her three sisters.

Certainly no children ever had a happier childhood than we had, and though often times were bad, tenants did not pay, the country was disturbed and murders committed, nothing clouded the sunshine of our lives.

The Fleming family lived comfortably in big house style, killing and curing their pigs, salting bullocks and butchering sheep.

Eighteen milch cows always, which meant masses of milk, cream, and butter, all of the best ... The yard teemed with poultry, ducks, geese and turkeys, endless chickens, and of course eggs ... The most lovely walled garden I was ever in. Masses of fruit ... peaches, plums, figs, cherries, every kind of apples and pears, and quantities of strawberries and gooseberries etc. Plenty of everything of the best, but only plain homely cooking, large honest joints every day, lavish and wasteful.

One of the Fleming sisters later wrote of the perfect summers of her childhood, of

stealing in bare feet and nothing but my nightdress on, taking the house keys off the nail where they always hung – letting myself out by the greenhouse, running across the garden and tennis ground and out into the lawn. The glory and beauty of the early morning at 5 o'clock, the long grass soaked with dew and dripping trees, and the glinting sunshine over it all. The silence and unbroken calm.

The household dogs were remembered by the sisters in later life and their names recorded – Nellie-Bly the black spaniel, hated because of her smell, Jet, 'the jolliest gamiest little dog', Gee-Jack, not so much loved, Bruno, Bessie's water spaniel who went to church and lay under her feet, and Joan, the red setter, the best shooting dog that ever lived. ('She had puppies off and on who always vanished at once. We used to milk her into egg-cups hoping for a delicious drink.')

We also had a tortoise, the dullest of pets, whom we scrubbed with soap and water; and endless canaries, detestable birds. They flew about the dining room during meals, perched on our heads and shoulders and walked about the table eating butter and crumbs.

Cocky, the cockatoo who ended up in Farmhill, started life at New Court.

There were hymns sung every evening and charitable works. ('Bessie was splendid about visiting the poor.') There were regattas and sailing to the islands, picnics, and tennis. The house was nearly always full of guests.

And when they came, they came to stay. Such things as 'week-ends' were unknown then. No, when they came, it was for anything from a fortnight to a month, generally a month.

The Flemings' second cousin, Edith Somerville, (who was also my grandfather's second cousin) lived a few miles away in Castletownshend. Versatile at music, painting and horse-dealing, as well as writing, Edith was regarded as the Renaissance woman of West Cork. Among her most success-ful paintings is a fine portrait of my Great Aunt Hatta lying on a couch with a black kitten. The picture is still in the posses-sion of her grandson, my Cousin Brendan. The Flemings gave her enough money for the painting to pay for her rail fare to Galway and her keep for several weeks at Ross House where her friend Violet Martin lived, her literary collaborator under the pseudonym, Martin Ross.

But snobberies were subtle, and it is evident from Edith's correspondence with Martin that she looked down on the Fleming 'girlies'. Like so many members of her family, Edith was a snob. Those acquaintances who did not form part of the 'tribe' – the four or five families who lived in big houses in Castletownshend – were known as 'suburbans'. When the Somervilles went to church, they sat in the front pew, as befitted their rank, while inferior souls sat behind them. This custom continued well into living memory.

The impression given by Edith in her letters is that the Flemings, 'surburbans' in spite of cousinhood, were inconvenient socially, four girls whose accents were considered more provincial than those of Castletownshend. Edith imitated them on paper. 'Bessie,' (with a luscious sigh of loving remembrance) 'I *do* think that Eedith was far the prittiest in the room!' (sic)

The Fleming girls tended not to be invited to parties, or to be asked to dances where there were not enough male partners, although they might attend inferior gatherings. Edith wrote scornfully to Martin how 'Yesterday thirty of the uncircumcised were here for tennis – very exhausting.'

In spite of their accents, their absence at parties and Edith's patronage, the 'girlies' all managed to find husbands. But there were difficulties in the way. In a letter to Violet Martin written in 1887 Edith described a Fleming courtship:

Great agitation prevails at New Court just now – 'A young Man
. . . is very fond of our little girlie Bessie' – a most rank Galoot,
I may observe Richard O'Grady by name. There is division
amongst the girlies – Bessie and Susie loving him and the other
two abhorring him (with reason). Our people went there this
week and said the excitement was at fever height. Mother . . .
was 'in her glory' – a mixture of airy badinage combined with
the most searching cross examination had the effect of bringing
to light the minutest details . . . One of the girlies was sent into
the drawing room to do gooseberry, and there she found them,
my dear, sitting on a window seat, looking at each other, roaring
and crying – I naturally asked why – Mother said, 'Oh I don't
know, me dear, Love, I suppose.' I hear the last scene before he
left New Court was harrowing in the extreme. He went into the
yard and sat down on a water barrel, and weeping, refused to
pack his clothes. It seems he has – as yet – said nothing official,
and Mrs Fleming wanted to send him off in order that absence
might screw up his courage in writing, as he doesn't dare speak.
I wish I could tell you all the facts – they are unspeakably funny
– but I haven't time.

I should be grateful to Mr O'Grady for never screwing up
his courage to propose to Bessie.

Old Mrs Fleming, my great grandmother, who aroused
Edith's scornful mimicry by referring to her daughters as her
girlies, was a gossip with a good fund of local information. In
1895 Edith Somerville and Violet Martin wrote their master-
piece, *The Real Charlotte*. It was generally known that the
character of Charlotte was based on that of Emily Herbert,
who, poor woman, was detested by many. After the book's
publication Mrs Fleming shook Edith by bringing up the

subject. Details that Edith and Martin had written as fiction turned out to be fact.

Another letter to Violet Martin tells how

Mrs F . . . began to speak of *The Real Charlotte* – 'Tell me, Edith, how did you know Emily Herbert had had a love affair?' I said we didn't know, but we had invented it. 'Well, Edith, all that you wrote is *pairfectly true*!' She then went on to say that there had been an attorney named Raymond . . . of whom Emily was deeply enamoured. He was married to a good little nonentity (Mrs Lambert!!) and to her Emily paid high court till she died, and then siege was laid to Raymond, but, as in our inspired work, in vain, and so the matter ended. Isn't it extraordinary? Even aweful. Also they say it is an undoubted fact she steamed open letters that belonged to someone else!

I remember Edith Somerville visiting Farmhill in the late thirties at the time she received an honorary degree from Trinity College. After a nursery education, she was justifiably proud at becoming a doctor, and insistent that she should be addressed as such. (When she died, her doctor's gown, together with her hunting whip was laid on her coffin.) However, my grandfather, who was ten years older, was permitted to go on calling her Cousin Edith, and they got on famously. Other people found her a terrifying old lady.

Like my grandfather, my grandmother, Bessie Fleming, married twice. The first time was to an old fellow named Horace Townsend who died of old age soon after. Then she went on a pilgrimage to the Holy Land where she met the Reverend William Somerville-Large, widowed like herself. They fell in love instantly, so much so, that at the end of the pilgrimage they brought back two huge flagons of Jordan water in which to baptise their future children, my father and uncles. After they were emptied these flagons went on display in my grandfather's study, together with other souvenirs of his courtship – brown views of Palestine, Egypt and the Holy Places, dotted all over the walls in Oxford frames.

The Canon had a happy second marriage which produced three sons, an active career in a succession of Gothic churches and a long second widowerhood spent in the company of his brothers and sons at Farmhill under the domination of Miss Moore. The food she provided might have left something to be desired: 'Lunch. Brains for Canon. Stewed steak. Rice pudding.' But Anthony Trollope has witnessed how pleasant life could be for a comfortably-off clergyman. My grandfather kept busy communicating with his wives and writing his memories.

What a wedding it was . . . I remember well Annie's handsome face and high colour, with the love light in her eye, but perhaps best of all the magnificence of my own clothes – Eton jacket, white waistcoat, the suit made by the best Cork tailors, Keene and Tumbull, much favoured by military men, and the tight, smart, patent leather boots which began the long life history of corns. But I *was* vain of myself that day.

His faith was secure, and it seems unfair that God should punish such a good and faithful servant by closing his life in the mists of Alzheimer's.

If you were thrifty, sober, sane and Protestant, and wanted to stay in the area of Cork, it was difficult to find an occupation, especially since families tended to be large. There were not enough jobs to go around among younger sons. Many left Cork for Canada, the United States, Australia, and to a lesser extent South Africa. The descendants of such emigrants occasionally get in touch with me. Last year a Somerville visited me, whose ancestor had gone to Melbourne in 1828. His genes were strong; after eight generations in Australia his descendant was the image of a cousin whose people have remained in West Cork.

I dread receiving letters from distant countries which open typically: 'I found your book in the Auckland Library ... may I point out a mistake on page 89.' Many seek information about a Somerville, Townsend, Fleming or some other members of West Cork families. The latest is from a Somerville in New Zealand who writes from 'Drishane' a house named after the big Somerville house in Castletownshend where Cousin Edith lived. He asks for news of 'Grandad', a distant cousin of ours who lived in a house in West Cork called 'The Prairie', and emigrated to Australia at the turn of the century. I can only confirm that he was, in the words of my own grandad, 'a wild reckless squireen' who sold his estates and eloped to Australia with his cook, leaving his wife and children behind in Liverpool.

4

Illaunslea

IN 1933 MY FATHER decided to buy an island. Twenty bare acres, ribbed with granite, did not amount to much and there were no amenities whatsoever. But as far as my father was concerned he had acquired a piece of heaven.

The island was called Illaunslea and was situated on the north shore of the Kenmare River in County Kerry. The 'river' was not a river at all, merely a long fiord. I have been told that successive Lords Lansdowne who owned a great stretch of land along its banks, called it a river, in legal documents, in order to safeguard their fishing rights.

Illaunslea was just off Parknasilla, 'the place of the willows', part of the estate attached to the Great Southern Hotel. In the early years of the century, the Great Southern and Western Railway Company built or enlarged a series of hotels in beautiful places. At Parknasilla their flagship enterprise was a huge Victorian edifice overlooking the long stretch of the Kenmare River westward through lines of mountains towards a luminous distance touched by the setting sun and signalled by a group of gannet-clouded rocks known as the Bull, the Cow and the Calf. There was a classical symmetry about the scene. Substitute a Roman temple for the gables of the hotel and you had a view by Claude Lorraine, an image of harmony between man and nature, touched with melancholy which may have had something to do with the forecast of rain.

The Parknasilla Hotel, with its golf course, boating facilities and nearby seas and rivers leaping with fish, was designed to appeal to affluent tourists. However, when my father first paid a visit there in 1926 he was not impressed. 'We called in at the hotel for tea and I remember thinking what a ghastly place it was.' Anything that offered a modicum of comfort was anathema to him. But he remembered the beauty of the mountains and sea and returned five years later. Soon he would live there whenever he had a moment to spare in his busy life. He would buy an island. He would convert it into a paradise.

His diary reflects the joy he felt from the very first moment he saw it. In the spring of 1932 Mrs Power, the manageress of Parknasilla, took my parents on a tour of the islands on the periphery of the hotel. Illaunslea

> consisted then of rocks covered with heather and gorse and valleys between them clothed deeply in rank grass with bog in most places. It was not alluring by any means, but then the views in every direction were wonderful and the anchorages and sheltered waters perfect, so we came away determined, if possible, to buy the island.

'We' meant 'I'. My mother would come to love the island and its inconveniences, but my father was king.

Purchase was not easy. The directors of the railway company were unhappy about breaking up their little empire, particularly anything beside their property at Parknasilla 'the apple of their myopic eyes'. At one time they had considered building some sort of bridge or causeway to the island and including it as a hazardous stretch of their golf course. In addition they feared that if they sold off part of their land, a rival hotel enterprise might start up. Considering my father's future enterprise in the hotel business in County Wicklow, they had some justification for their misgivings.

But in 1932 after long haggling he persuaded them of his good intentions and they parted with Illaunslea, together with another sliver of an island known as Illaungar. He was given a lease for a hundred and fifty years for which he paid fifty pounds, together with an extra twelve guineas for registering the sale.

He was by no means the first rich newcomer to be attracted to this spectacular region. In the late nineteenth century the area was described in Murray's *Guide* as 'a wooded oasis of gentlemen's residences'. The land around Parknasilla had once belonged to a family named Bland whose ancestor acquired huge tracts of County Kerry in the carve up of forfeited estates at the end of the seventeenth century. Before the Land Acts the Blands owned forty thousand acres along the Kenmare River and a castle called Derryquin which was burnt in the Civil War; its ruin looms over the hotel golf course. When sometime in the 1880s the estate was broken up, its most spectacular island, Garnish, was acquired by the Dunraven family, while Robert Graves' grandfather, the Bishop of Limerick, bought Parknasilla, Derryquin Castle and various little islands, including Illaunslea. Later the Graves sold all their land to the Great Southern Railway Company.

Bishop Graves was famous for writing a sentimental ballad named 'Father O'Flynn' said to be based on the parish priest of Kilcrohane across the Kenmare River. This coy exercise in ecumenism proved to be immensely popular sung beside many an upright piano. When he owned Parknasilla, he installed a man called Downey on our island, which for a time was known as Downey's Island. Downey had to pay the Bishop six pence a year, a rent later increased to five shillings which my father continued to pay to the railway people. Downey's grandson was one of a team of workmen brought in by my father to carry out his plans for developing the island as a haven for sailing boats.

His ideas differed from those of his super-rich neighbours who were less interested in sailing than in gardens. Several millionaires had been attracted to the region by the fact that there was hardly any frost and with the aid of many thousands of pounds it was possible to impose a ferny tropical jungle on top of the bogs and rock of Kerry.

A nineteenth-century English gardener named William Robinson was responsible for this particular grandiose enthusiasm. Robinson gave his name to a form of gardening which, not only took advantage of natural landscapes, but inspired gentlemen gardeners to plant hosts of exotic plants in a way that looked as if they had grown there naturally, instead of being lugged over from New Zealand or Chile. There was nowhere better to exploit the Robinsonian idea than the south-west corner of Ireland beside the Gulf Stream. Megalomaniacal gardeners arrived there regularly, bought properties, shifted rocks and planted trees.

On the Kenmare River to the south of us, across the water, the Lords Lansdowne developed their bare acres at Dereen, first by planting thousands of sycamore, ash and evergreen pines, and later, when areas of shelter had been created, filling in spaces with rhododendrons, myrtles, embothriums and tree ferns. In 1903 King Edward VII and Queen Alexandra made the long journey to Dereen to visit the current Lord Lansdowne, who had spent much of his working life as a diplomat. He seems to have made sure of being posted to many different parts of the world where there were interesting plants and shrubs that liked a lot of rain. After admiring the crinodendrons, hydrangeas, hoherias, cordyline palms and phormiums, their majesties walked with their umbrellas on a damp peaty path through a green tunnel planted with tree ferns, subsequently named King's Oozy.

Around our island other subtropical gardens flourished in the drizzle. On Garnish Island the 3rd Earl of Dunraven took advantage of a wood of indigenous sessile oak, some limestone ridges and sheltered glens to grow huge magnolias, azaleas and a long avenue of *Dicksonia antarctica,* or tree ferns. At Reenafera Colonel Hartley was growing cabbage palms and disgusting gunnera whose leaves like giant rhubarb were said to be bigger than anyone else's. On Rossdohan, yet another island, Colonel Samuel Heard not only grew *Dicksonia antarctica,* but another rare silver tree fern, *Cyathea dealbata* which is said to have once covered the globe millions of years ago.

Colonel Heard died in 1921 and a volume of Curtis's *Botanical Magazine* was dedicated to him in acknowledgement of all the giant rarities that spread over Rossdohan. Two years later his eccentric house with its glazed veranda enclosed in stained glass was destroyed in the spate of burnings that took place in the area during the Troubles.

Like Uncle Bris, Colonel Heard had been an army surgeon. My father was also a surgeon, and there may have been some medical reason for him to refer to the Colonel as a certified lunatic. Perhaps he was jealous since he had come late to the game of creating island paradises. Colonel Heard had acquired

Rossdohan in 1870 and, like Illaunslea, it had started off as a stretch of bog and rock surrounded by water. My father had fifty years to make up. But he was not interested in Robinsonian theories and ideas. Apart from planting a few thousand trees, he would leave most of the business of gardening to my mother.

What he really liked was fishing and sailing. And from the Kenmare River there was perfect sailing in every direction. He wrote: 'I wonder why more yachts do not sail this coast? It is incredibly lovely. More beautiful by far than anything I have seen in England and studded with islands and good harbours.'

First of all, Illaunslea had to be civilised, and he set about the task with gusto. His first priority was to lay down deep moorings, make slips and build a boathouse with specially laid rails and sleepers to take the fleet which he would assemble. A swaying drawbridge would link the harbour with the land. He was so preoccupied with nautical matters that the actual taming of the island itself was almost an afterthought. The land, which was part of an area known as Ballybog, had to be drained and planted.

Lord Lansdowne had employed forty people to shift the landscape at Dereen; my father did things on a smaller scale and used only half a dozen men. Equipment was painstakingly carried over from the mainland in rowing boats. Footpaths were laboriously hacked out through briars and along the rock ridges, trees began to be planted and everywhere drains were dug. Beside each drain a hedge of royal fern, *Osmunda regalis,* would grow up, its bronze leaves unfurling and rising to a height of six feet.

A hut in which the Downeys had once lived was re-roofed and nearby an Elsan, a basic flushless lavatory, disinfected by

Lysol whose smell wafted over the rocks and heather, was installed in another smaller hut. A railway signal was erected outside; the joke was that it should be raised when occupied.

Phil and I first saw the island in 1933. We motored down with my father, never having left Dublin before. My mother travelled separately in a van borrowed from my uncle, while my father took us together with Nanny Somers and Harry Michael, one of his friends. Crushed in the back of his Ford, we wondered what to expect. We had been told a lot about the island and our reading had given us some idea of monkeys and pirates. The journey was long, and halfway we stopped in Frank McCourt's Limerick where Phil and Peter, children of privilege, were given a substantial lunch.

The dining room in Cruise's Hotel in O'Connell Street was gloomy, lightened a little by the curved mirror over the massive sideboard which was dotted with cruets. There was an aspidistra in a brass pot. The menu was not unlike food at Farmhill and I ate a large helping of brown beef in brown gravy that shone like shoe leather, followed by prunes and custard.

Ten miles on at Adare it was realised that a mistake had been made.

'I'm feeling sick.'

My father, who was driving did not reply.

'Please, Daddy . . .'

He did not stop, but opened the sliding roof. By standing on the back seat I could push my head out into the rushing stream of air until another bump in the road brought grief. There was a sort of justice that the contents of my stomach emptied over his head.

'Dash it, you've ruined my shirt and jacket.'

'I didn't mean it, Daddy.'

'I should hope not!' Nanny Somers piped up.

The car came to a reluctant halt and while he threw his shirt and jacket in the boot, and looked for something else to wear, Nanny Somers rubbed me down with grass. She was making the noise generally written *tsk tsk*, anticipating for the first time her future nightmare task of seeing that neither Phil nor I disappeared off the island and drowned. Meanwhile I could tell my father was annoyed.

'Next time you are going to get sick at least have the courtesy to tell me.'

While he might not suffer directly from car sickness, he was as sick as a parrot every time he embarked on a boat. He might have been more sympathetic.

We were entering a different world beyond Limerick. A white road, little traffic and barefoot children. Burly figures of farmers armed with sticks and lonely farmhouses on the sides of misty hills. Desolate Rathkeale, and Newcastle West. The sort of towns remembered with nostalgia by John Betjeman:

> Look out where yon cabins grow smaller to smallest
> Straw-thatched and one-storeyed and soon to come down ...

There was a fair at Castleisland and the wide main street was jammed with carts, horses, donkeys and assorted livestock. Men in gumboots and tattered old coats were tangling. As the car wound its way through the congestion, we could hear the strong musical voices.

'I'm telling you she's as sound as a bell.'

'Arrah, get out of that. I wasn't born yesterday.'

'Is there a deal?'

We drove past houses in the Kerry Gothic style with gables, curling wooden eaves and fretwork bargeboards. I glimpsed fuchsia hedges and was beginning to feel sick again. By the time we reached Killarney dusk was wrapping the woods and obscuring the vulgar mauve of the rhododendrons. I fell asleep as the car twisted over the mountains past black-faced sheep, their fleeces gleaming with raindrops, and through Moll's Gap.

The rain had ceased and stars were out when we arrived at a pier. This was the Oysterbed Pier which had been built at a time when a large population of farmers and fishermen lived in the area. Successive waves of emigration had left it largely unused. When we saw it by day we could make out a few broken hulks, spars and old lobster pots, the rotting remains of a once thriving economy. The oysters after which it was named had died of some disease.

My father was shaking hands with a figure who emerged out of the darkness – Jimmy Sullivan, who would take us over in an open rowing boat. We waited for the van to arrive on the pier with my mother, two maids and various animals, dogs, a cat in a basket, a load of mattresses and a crate filled with six hens.

Bruin, who we nicknamed 'garden of roses' was the chief reason we had not travelled in the van. Even before we departed there was a suspicion that his powerful stench might induce car sickness in me. Bernadette, one of the maids, had suffered instead. But my mother was kinder than my father, and her car had stopped frequently on the way down.

No one considered life jackets in those days, and my father's warning had to suffice as far as safety was concerned.

'Now, boys. I don't want you to mess around, and always remember that the sea can be dangerous and unforgiving.'

Bruin had been to the island before, and the dogs leapt into the boat, followed by the passengers, the luggage, cardboard boxes filled with food, the mattresses and the laundry wrapped in brown paper. My father and Jimmy Sullivan rowed in the darkness against a strong tide; each dip of the oars created a fiery trail of phosphorescence.

The slow journey over the water under the stars took less than ten minutes. Before the boat could nudge on to the island there was a huge splash as Bruin had missed the landfall and tumbled into the sea. We disembarked in the dark, the adults carrying luggage up the wet and slippery rocks.

We took a long time getting to bed. Tents had to be erected for the maids and my father's friend, Harry. By candlelight mattresses were covered with sheets. We slept in Downey's hut en famille – my parents, ourselves, Nanny Somers, the dogs and the cat, still in her basket.

Next morning Phil and I ran down over the rocks and heather to the harbour, heedless of Nanny Somers' cries. The tide was out and there was a smell of mud and the strong distinct smell of the sea that comes from exposed seaweed. The day was windless, the water unruffled and a heron took off from a rock covered with two kinds of seaweed, shining ruby fronds and the stuff that was kept floating by little bladders that could be burst with a satisfying pop.

Here was the beginning of our long love affair with Illaunslea. Over the years many elements on sea and land would contribute to the enchantment which we would discover little by little as we grew older. There would be the seals; nearly always when we went out a head would be in view like a rock until we caught sight of a satisfied whiskered face which my father said reminded him of his bank manager. In May seals gathered on Illaungar, the young ones woolly and white.

The porpoises would find us when we sailed, tacking westward towards the Bull and the Calf. Gannets would fly up the river thirty or forty miles from their nesting sites on the Bull and the Skelligs. Pale eyes beneath tobacco stained heads would view the rippling mackerel before the dive and splash.

There would be the sailing and all the fishing, and the sea creatures lying off shore visible in the clear water, the scallops at the bottom of the clear water off Garnish, the shrimps, the starfish, and sea urchins. In summer when it was hot, the Portuguese men-of-war would float in, carrying their knotted bead curtains. We would sail among the basking sharks, their fins raised out of the water, their great open mouths five feet across. There would be the time when we found ourselves in the middle of a crowd of killer whales with black and white clown faces and George Formby grins, who were swooping up the river in unison and overtook us, rubbing their bodies against our boat, their tails as big as sails.

The dolphins were smaller than the killer whales, but they were more insistent, tormenting us with their jovial bullying. We already knew of two particularly well known dolphins, which lived in the harbours at Baltimore and Schull in West Cork and were generally considered a nuisance. The one in Schull had a liking for anchor chains. Once when we had sailed into Schull we could plainly see him through the clear water slipping a loop of the anchor chain around his nose, lifting the anchor off the bottom and making away with it. The people of Schull used to find their boats all over the place wherever their dolphin chose to drag them. In order to discourage him they wound large hooks to their mooring chains and we could see that his back was covered with scars.

The dolphins that chose to stay near Illaunslea one whole

summer were a pod, six in number, and at first we were frightened. When we ventured out past Illaungar we knew they
would be somewhere near; they would catch sight of us from
wherever they were cruising, usually off Sherkey Island, and
come rushing over the water to greet us. They would not leave
us alone. They were not interested in the bigger boats, but
seemed to think that our dinghies, just their size, were fellow
creatures. They jostled us as they swam beneath us; or they
would leap from the water to look down at us out of their
piggy eyes before plunging back into the water. We did not
like this at all; there was less favourable publicity about dolphins
in those days.

It took time to get used to six squeaking dolphins with their
curious fixed smiles, but as the days passed of a summer when
the sun was shining every day, we learned slowly that we had
nothing to fear. We would go out looking for them and wait
for them to come running over like the dogs. If we had known
more, we might have dived in among them, as people do nowadays, but we kept in the boats and lowered our sails as they
circled, swooped and dived and rubbed their backs on the
keels. They would stay around us, and gradually became interested in the bigger boats. I remember one moonlit night
particularly, returning in the *Memphis* from the Oysterbed Pier,
and how they escorted us leaping about the bow, hissing and
clicking as they breathed, six huge shining shapes covered with
rippling phosphorescent water.

But the day came when they were not there; some fool with
a gun, may he rot, who regarded them merely as large fish,
shot one, and the rest departed instantly, never to return. The
Kenmare River was an emptier place after that.

5

Kerry Rain

IN THAT FIRST summer accommodation on the island was rudimentary. The sleeping accommodation consisted of Downey's hut with its three bunks, some tents with camp beds and the boathouse in which my father slept in a hammock. In spite of this a number of my father's friends were invited down to Illaunslea after he had given them flowery ideas about the joys of island living. They came in instalments, not knowing what to expect. Their misgivings may have begun when their cars arrived at the Oysterbed Pier, since the only way they could attract our attention was by blaring their horns. Over on the island we might hear them faintly like elfin horns of fairy land, but often we were away somewhere and they would be left for hours as the evening drew in.

Often people arrived late, having driven the long way down from Dublin. In that first summer Uncle Paddy arrived with Aunt Grace at midnight in pitch darkness. My father recorded in his diary:

Pad drove to the Oysterbed Pier, luckily stopping in time as there was nothing to protect him from going over the edge, and then started exercising his lungs to their best capacity. The men on a large 90-ton private schooner, thinking apparently that their owner was being attacked, set off and rowed with all haste to the pier. Pad, Grace, his dog and dirty kit bag immediately got on board and requested to be rowed to the island. Pad steered in what he thought was the right direction until they hit some rocks. They scrambled over these in the dark, and fighting their way against all odds arrived by the merest luck at the house. They might just as easily have landed on Illaungar where they would have had to spend the night without shelter if they had succeeded in avoiding falling off one of the cliffs into the sea.

Other guests that year were a couple named Briggs who did not have their own transport. My father went down to Cork and brought them back to Parknasilla in a gale. 'They were convinced that our accommodation consisted of a comfortable house with the usual offices, and we had not the heart to tell them the worst, so we gave them tea at the hotel instead. We ultimately went out in the *Memphis* to the island.' The *Memphis* was a large open rowing boat. It never occurred to him to have a boat fitted with some sort of canopy for shelter. When it rained passengers got wet, and so did the bread, the rugs, all those sheets wrapped in brown paper, and Bruin. When Bruin was wet, he stank.

Gleefully my father continued his account of the wretched Briggs' visit. 'When they saw the tiny cottage in the wind and rain, the horror was so painful that we couldn't watch it. If it hadn't been an island, they would have disappeared during the night.'

Over the years there would be other unfortunate arrivals, like that of a Swedish doctor and his wife who also arrived at night. There was barely enough water to float the boat so

Betzie and Sven were hustled into it and pushed out. Betzie was dressed in couturier clothes; deciding not to ruin her beautiful shoes, she waded down through stones and mud in her fine silk stockings. My father informed her that she was extremely lucky since the boat might have easily stuck in the mud, in which case they would have had to wait three or four hours in the dark for the tide to float it.

Once the guests had arrived, keeping them happy would always be a problem. The weather could not be relied on. My mind is filled with memories of blissful days when the sun shone and we were surrounded by deep blue sea, or the clear water in the creeks beside us which the poet John Montague compared to rhinestone. Above us would be blue sky, and in the distance the odd lazy white cloud floating over the mountains. There were blue mountains and green mountains, and above the nearest village of Sneem a large hill called the Giant's Seat with shadows running across its bare surface. Further away the dome of Hungry Hill was visible and on certain days the craggy lines of the Macgillicuddy's Reeks could be seen, one behind the other, guarding Killarney. But somewhere there the clouds assembled; on the finest day you would always glimpse one or two in the distance, menacing, like the sight of a tank in a country that is being invaded.

How many summer regattas have I seen with men in their soaking best suits, standing under downpours on packed piers watching for boats hidden in torrents of mist? Rain differed in quality. The summer rain could be endured because it was not constant. It greeted you in August, around the time the mackerel came in, falling loudly on leaves as you sheltered under trees. Huge drops hit the arbutilon and agapanthus and the American Pillar roses. Then the sun came out hot and the ground steamed as if we were in Indonesia.

That sort of rain, easy come, easy go, was fine. The other stuff threatened to make life unendurable – the misty drizzle coming in clouds blown from the west that gave the impression it would never go away. It could rain all day and clear in the evenings when the setting sun shone on the diamond drops all around you with the promise of cessation. Then, in the early hours of the following morning, you could hear the tap-tap on the window that indicated another bad interlude and there would be more waiting for the sun which would place us in Paradise again. But a Kerry drizzle could last for eighteen days.

The odd storm brought variety. In 1934, the second year Phil and I went down to Kerry, there was a particularly fierce summer storm. Downey's hut had a corrugated roof and the noise frightened me, so that I climbed into the bed of Mary the cook, seeking comfort from her vast warm body, and earning contempt from my brother and the rest of the family.

I remember the lashing winds and rain and how our little world vanished in mist and spray. The weather got worse and for a couple of days most of us crowded wet and shivering in the hut playing Snap and Beggar my Neighbour. (In later years wet days would be paced by Racing Demon, Canasta and Irish Monopoly – Kimmage and Crumlin at the cheap end, Ailsbury Road and Shrewsbury Road the most expensive buys.) But during that storm of 1934 my father went out and he was literally in his element. Exhilarated, he put on boots and oilskins, and with a few of his more faithful followers stepped into the raging tempest like pilgrims in the hymn. There was swelling water, grey wind, rain sprinting sideways and noise to enjoy. Giant waves covered the whole island in drenching spray. 'I have never conceived that the wind could blow so hard,' he wrote later.

The local correspondent of the *Cork Examiner* described the storm in an emotional article, telling of yachts dragging their anchors, boats torn from their moorings, and how my father rescued one boat in particular.

The safety of the motor yacht *Spray* is due to the exertions of Somerville-Large and his party who . . . boarded the *Spray*, unfurled the jib sail, and with the aid of their motor boat towed her into safety into Garnish harbour.

My father was gratified at this account, only critical that the *Examiner*'s correspondent had declared that the Somerville-Large yacht 'kept up steam all night'.

'Fool! No one in a private yacht has kept up steam for years.'

The writer was eloquent in his description of how my father rescued other yachts carelessly dragging their anchors which were drifting in his vicinity during the gale. 'Old seamen say it was the worst storm they ever remember in Garnish harbour, which is considered one of the safest harbours in Ireland, being protected on all sides by large woods. It is, indeed, most fortunate that there was no loss of life.' The writer concluded that this happy circumstance was entirely due to the efforts of my father. 'Those onlookers from the shore were loud in their praise of the daring of Dr Somerville-Large and his party.'

'Inaccurate,' said my father. 'Ridiculous. Drivel conjured up in the man's vivid and probably alcoholic imagination.'

He soon discovered that the *Examiner* correspondent was one of the most powerful personalities of Sneem, the village nearest to the island, situated three miles from the Oysterbed. J.J. Sheehan was the proprietor of a business near the bridge which was half shop and half pub. I have written before about the magic of J.J.'s store. They do not have shops like that any more, with hobnailed boots, and gumboots, socks and sticky seaman's jackets that had to be torn apart, all hanging from the ceiling, while every corner got crowded out with spinners, hooks, coils of wire and rope, sides of bacon, tins of galvanised paint, creosote, chainsaws, anchor chains, Elsan disinfectant, John West's salmon and hunks of smoked ling. There were women's coats in puce and Kerry green, dresses, hats and petticoats.

Sneem soon became an extremely important port of call for us, and J.J.'s shop was frequently visited. Very soon we were making regular visits into the interior where J.J. sat in the snug, wearing his crushed brown hat stuck with fishing flies, smoking his pipe and retailing the latest gossip. He gave ginger beer to Phil and me, while he provided our elders with stronger drink and regaled them with recent scandal, being delighted to be the very first to tell the news of the doings of the divorcee staying in the Great Southern.

Gradually we became acquainted with Sneem. My father might preach self-sufficiency, but we were no Blasket Islanders and, whether he liked it or not, we had to make excursions to 'the continent of Ireland', to Sneem or Kenmare, for supplies.

Squeezed between mountains and sea, Sneem was divided into two small squares, each with a muddy green linked by a stone bridge. There were two butchers and two churches.

The village was small and intimate and the goats, sheep and geese grazing the greens had their own names. My father wrote in his diary:

> all the shops are full of ample ladies in black shawls who never seem to buy but just block the entrances and it seems to afford considerable surprise if you express a desire for anything but alcoholic refreshment (18 pubs). It takes considerable time to receive attention and needs a demonstration of patience and back chat that would put Job to shame.

Prominent residents of Sneem included Lena Fitzgerald at the Green House. Our favourite.

'Now, my darlings, what would you like?'

She had jars of bulls' eyes and strings of licorice, fizz, boiled fruit gums, acid drops and local bars of faintly stale chocolate. She never allowed us to pay. She was a tall stout lady, always dressed in black, and sometimes from her room upstairs with the piano, you could hear her strong operatic voice singing over the village operatic airs and patriotic songs and 'Danny Boy'.

Winnie Hurley ruled her bar with the air of an abbess. Much of her time was spent exchanging heavy banter with the colonels and majors who chose to live in the area, in large damp houses, from where they would emerge to fish or shoot or come into Sneem for their whiskey – their medicine, they called it.

In one of the houses surrounding the larger green, invariably spotted with grazing donkeys and geese, lived the Christiansons, descendants from a Norwegian brought to Ireland together with a quantity of Norwegian pine to build

Lord Dunraven's boathouse, a vast building like a church. The Christiansons had lost their Nordic memories and gained musical Kerry voices. One of them still lives there.

In spite of what he considered misdirected efforts in creating a tropical garden on Garnish Island, my father approved of Lord Dunraven and his family, the Wyndham Quins, because ultimately they put yachts before gardens, and spent a large part of their considerable fortune derived from English coal mines on commissioning one lavish yacht after another. One Lord Dunraven had nearly defeated Sir Thomas Lipton in the America's Cup.

Sneem was situated on what was known even then as the Ring of Kerry, part of a picturesque circuit that took a very few tourists in cars through the town along the twisting stony road that bordered the magnificent Kerry coastline towards Cahirciveen, where Daniel O'Connell had lived, Waterville and beyond. In 1880 Murray's handbook had described Sneem as 'a poor little town, or rather village, near the mouth of the Sneem river, and embosomed amidst rocks and mountains'. That description could pass for the 1930s. Cars were few enough to be stared at as they went by. The mail car passed through every day, but otherwise most people used bicycles or donkeys and the little carts known as low-backed cars to make their way to the creamery.

Our privileged family could drive our cars into the village for supplies, but usually my father preferred to visit the hard way. After we had bought our needs for the next week we would walk down to the pier under the bridge to where the *Memphis* waited, often in rain. The journey back to the island along the snaking Sneem River to the open sea had to be taken on the falling tide.

'Keep still, you're rocking the boat.'

'For God's sake, someone hold on to Bruin.'

Along the river were small but violent whirlpools and currents, and there were rocks which jutted out of the water at low tide. The engine might stop.

'Watch out!'

'Use the oars.'

The rocky Kerry hills in the distance always looked serene.

My family loved sailing and my grandfather's reminiscences are full of sailing expeditions. At the beginning of the century Uncle Phil and Uncle Bris had shared a vast iron yawl named the *Vindex*; built in 1863, she weighed forty-six tons and was sailed with the aid of four uniformed, moustached seamen. When they were not polishing the brasswork, handling the ropes or putting up bunting on occasions like Queen Victoria's Jubilee, the crew of the *Vindex* took ladies and gentlemen on short day cruises around the coast of West Cork. The gentlemen wore sailor hats and Panamas, while the ladies wore handbags clipped to their waists and huge hats held on against the south-west wind with hat pins. They posed for photographs under the sails and sat in deckchairs, since there was no cockpit.

'So that's why they are called deckchairs!'

A photograph exists of my father wrapped in voluminous baby clothes and huge white bonnet in Uncle Bris's arms on the deck of the *Vindex*, so his yachting experience began early. Although he was regularly seasick, this did not deter his passion for boats. In the 1930s sailing large yachts, misnamed pleasure cruising, was a pastime that was going through its most uncomfortable phase. Accommodation was spartan. There were plenty of ropes to handle and none of the slick

Terylene sails, radar and aids to sailing and navigation that would come later. My father kept hired hands, but much of the work of sailing had to be done by friends and amateurs put to work as hard as any Jack Tar a century before, and pretending to be enjoying themselves.

My father set aside part of every summer to go cruising. Year after year, he went forth with his long-suffering friends and their wives.

'I want you to pull up the anchor,' he would nonchalantly ask a guest who had clambered on board. 'If you find mud on the chain, wash it off with the brush stowed forward.'

Once the yacht had cleared Garnish the fishing lines would be assembled. Soon those on board might be unlucky enough to be enduring Dursey Sound with its whiplash tides and uneven rollers. It took very bad weather for my father to turn back.

His log book doggedly noted the misery.

Foynes Harbour. Wednesday August 3. Never again. The banks are just mud of the foulest kind which is exposed in large quantities at low water and the views are most depressing.

Tarbert. Thursday August 4. Barometer 2.9.4. Continuous hard heavy rain with visibility falling from 9 miles to about half a mile. The winds S. of West of medium strength. I gave up at 7 a.m.

Tuesday 9 August – The boat rolled all night and I slept very little owing to the noise and the difficulty of staying in my bunk.

25 August. We started off with the intention of going to Eyries to look at a boat, but when half way across the Kenmare River the wind suddenly increased to a very great extent and the sea

became very dangerous. The tops of the big waves started breaking over us and hitting the mainsail. The punt filled in a few minutes, turned over the tow rope, which broke near the stern of the punt. It was tragic to see the beautiful new dinghy disappear. Meanwhile the wind was increasing and it was blowing very hard – I could not leave the tiller and the rest of the hands did not know how to handle the sails. Soon the water got into the cockpit and covered the floor of the cabin and we set all hands to the pump. Everyone except Mr Illingworth got very sick – the ladies of the party were stretched inside the cabin where everything – including ourselves – was soaking wet.

Still he persisted. He summed up his philosophy.

One of the great truths of life . . . A man will spend all he has on his yacht or buy anything required to put her in perfect trim without a complaint. But if his wife wants another maid in the house, he is quite prepared to raise Cain. Nothing could be more reasonable.

It seems extraordinary that not only did my father keep his friends and their wives but made more. Bully as he was, he had an extraordinary gift for friendship. The fact that he was known as the Skipper may have been an indication of the loyalty he invited. There was something mesmeric about his personality that persuaded friends and relations, sober doctors and professional men and women to join in his discomfort. Year after year they consented to become part of his entourage. They convinced themselves that the gamble for a day or two of sunshine on the island in my father's company made everything worth while.

When they agreed to go on a voyage with him, they were discouraged from bringing along their usual whiskey in order to keep their spirits up. On my father's boats, any passenger who needed a stiff drink had to go up with their bottle to the bow and listen to the disapproving remarks that carried from the cockpit behind them.

It is true that a few managed to stay on land. 'We found the shore party lolling about congratulating themselves that we had such a nice day for our sail. Callous lack of appreciation of another's difficulties is most galling.' Others got restless as they ran out of cigarettes or missed their regular newspapers. The most pathetic victim of island fever was my mother's sister. At best a nervous person, after two days Aunt Eileen was heard and seen going round to every able-bodied person on the island with tears running down her face crying, 'Please, please, get me out of here!'

Others escaped, ending up at the Parknasilla Hotel which had always invited my father's scorn. Those who had fled our island, as he planned to embark on yet another trip through the Dursey Sound and round the Mizen, might be glimpsed from the *Memphis* 'lolling' on the hotel lawn in deckchairs. 'Cripples!' They included our Swedish friends, Betzie and Sven; Betzie's sufferings from sea sickness were so acute that they were long remembered as exceptional.

Another desolate victim of *mal de mer* was Fraulein Finger, Phil's German governess, press-ganged into going along with 'a boatload of sick women' through Dursey Sound and around the Mizen to visit our relatives at Castletownshend.

'Fraulein slept in the floor and was greatly in the way,' my father recorded. 'But when on her feet she was useful.'

My father had to put up with regular mutineers. 'I see

Barney has given in,' he would mutter. 'Imbecile.' Or worse still, Barney might be glimpsed playing golf.

'Nothing better to do!' It was surprising how friends like Barney would return beeping their car horns on the Oysterbed Pier and sliding up the slippery rocks at the island harbour full of apologies. They knew that at best they would be put to work clearing away stones or slashing at tussocks covered with papery brown dead grass. Or, more likely, they would be expected to go off once again on a cruise in uncertain weather, prepared for wind and rain blowing for days on end.

But even my father recognised that if he was going to keep these craven people around him, he would have to offer them something more than a sodden tent in the way of comfort. The storm of 1934 galvanised him into laying plans for a proper house which could take in guests who could at least sleep and eat comfortably.

Winnie Hurley was related to a promising young architect named Michael Scott, who was at the start of a prestigious career which would include the Royal Institute of Architects' gold medal. Scott agreed to build something more substantial on the island than Downey's hut. There were difficulties and arguments over his designs which my father scornfully condemned as 'artistic'; his idea for going 'all Moorish' was scornfully rejected and instead he was instructed to make the interior of the house as nautical in feeling as possible. The total area was designed to take up the same amount of room as a small cargo ship.

For six months quantities of building materials were ferried over from the Oysterbed. They included the fittings of a dismantled ship, acquired to provide the requisite teak and mahogany with which to line the interior. This meant that in future when these nautical bits and pieces were installed, we would be grappling with ladders instead of stairs, ship's bunks, folding basins, lockers and every possible reminder of life at sea. When we were lying in one of those narrow damp bunks during a storm, we would listen to the wind and the rain and be thankful that all we lacked to convince us we were out at sea was the motion of rocking.

The house was completed by Easter, 1935. Scott had made the exterior unusually elegant with a sloping green tiled roof and verandas looking towards magnificent views. By this time the island itself was beginning to be tamed. Coral paths had been laid out, and thousands of newly planted trees stood knee high.

My father loved parties.

Dr. and Mrs C. Somerville-Large

will be happy if you can visit them

at Illaunslea Island on Saturday,

27th April, when their new residence

will be informally opened.

At Home, 3-30 p.m. to 7 p.m.   *Please reply to:*

Boats from the Oyster Bed Pier.   16 FITZWILLIAM PLACE.

For days before, men were rowed over to the island to erect the tent and the dancing platform, together with the tar barrel which would provide torchlight. They put up bunting that stretched from the window of the small bedroom across the valley to the rock overhanging the path to the bathing place. A wireless with a loudspeaker was installed outside the house and a bar was set up. The bar seat was improvised by the use of the new springboard that was due to be installed at the west end of the island from where we could dive into the freezing water which we constantly reminded ourselves was warmed by the Gulf Stream.

Provisions of all sorts were provided. The priority was drink, and after much consultation with J.J., it was thought that forty-two dozen bottles of stout and ales (Cairns, Bass and Guinness) would be enough as a basis for liquid refreshment. Whiskey would be provided for the gentlemen, and for the ladies there would be sherry and tea, and sandwiches. The bread would be brought down from Dublin where it had been made and already sliced by a cook in the Country Shop.

A travelling fiddler was hired, who guaranteed to play twenty-two different tunes and in addition there would be an accordionist and various vocalists who would play and sing for free.

To have an open air party in April was a considerable gamble which my father won. We woke in great excitement to sunshine and a fresh south-westerly breeze which held the flags horizontally. Long before 3.30 the crowds began to row over, some in their own boats, most ferried from the Oysterbed Pier. In addition to the locals from as far away as Tahilla and Blackwater Bridge, guests included a batch of majors and colonels and numerous friends who had been galvanised to make the long journey down from Dublin with the promise of new comfort. People from all over the neighbourhood, the schoolmaster and doctor, and O'Brien Corkery, whose wonderful emporium in Kenmare was superior even to that of J.J. There were men in blue Sunday suits and caps, and women with richly patterned dresses; J.J. in his role as the *Examiner*'s correspondent had it 'on good authority that the ladies of the party had bought their creations in Cork'. There were numerous children, who, like us, were determined to evade their parents or nursemaids.

As the afternoon wore on, boats continued to arrive with late-comers and down at the harbour the air was full of the gentle splash of oars. Already among the knots of blue-clad figures were many looking the worse for wear. Some were swaying and a few were singing to the fiddle and accordion. 'Hold your tongue, sir, hold your tongue!' one old man kept shouting if anyone interrupted his garrulous flow which threatened to drown the fiddle's squeak.

A ship's bell was rung and speeches began to flow. 'Ladies and gentlemen and my relatives,' Michael Scott began. He spoke briefly, in comparison to J.J. whose oration was noted by *The Kerryman*. (American papers please copy.)

As you know, Dr Large and his party rescued in a storm the R.Y. Squadron of Garnish Harbour . . . You also know that when the garage of the Earl of Dunraven was threatened with fire, the doctor formed a fire brigade and with his friends succeeded in saving the building from complete destruction with grave personal danger to himself and his friend . . . Those heroic deeds should be kept green in the history of South Kerry.

My father said later, 'I have rarely heard such involved and spontaneous rubbish.'

Phil and I had to perform star roles. Dressed in our best – glittering white shirts, grey shorts with snake buckles, we were provided with silver scissors. At a given signal we cut red ribbons and, watched by very many people and envious children, we piped up: 'Ladies and gentlemen, the house is now open.' Nanny retrieved the scissors and we were free to go, while she spent the rest of the day searching for us among the revellers.

The ladies went inside the house where they were served tea and sandwiches, pushed through the hatch into the living room by Bernadette. Later they went outside to inspect the garden, listen to the wireless and sip sherry. Then various privileged men moved inside into their place and were given whiskey.

Dancing began on the dancing platform, whose wooden planks had been used in the mixing of concrete, so that their surface was rough, in spite of liberal use of chalk powder. It was not enough, so my mother's face powder had to be added. Sedate country dancing, foursomes and reels, going backwards and forwards over the uneven boards, were varied by songs. Someone with a megaphone called out the names of prospective singers. A tenor trilled 'The Last Rose of Summer' which John McCormack had been singing half an hour ago over the wireless. Percy French ballads were sung, including 'The Mountains of Mourne', which swept down to the sea like the Kerry mountains around us and 'Phil the Fluter's Ball', which echoed some of the goings on that afternoon. Con Sullivan seemed to be inventing songs as he went along with much use of words like 'Parknasilla' and 'Skelligs'.

Con went on for a long time until he was howled down by a counter-chorus from the bar. Phil and I particularly applauded the blacksmith shouting, 'I am a Gay Caballero.'

The dancing, singing and drinking went on in the field as dignitaries and ladies continued to be entertained up at the house with sherry and whiskey, while the building was being inspected. Sam Sullivan, the builder, took them round in a slow funereal procession, glasses in hand. 'Gentlemen, this is the ceiling. Here is the floor.' The reporter from *The Kerryman* observed approvingly how

in the general layout of the residence one can observe the sailor mind, and one can guarantee both the residence and the island seaworthy, in the hands of a skilful navigator.

The colonels and their ladies left early but everyone else stayed on. At about six o'clock there were more speeches after Dr Fogarty got up on the table near the tent and declared that, as the local leader of the IRA, he was glad to assure us that whatever happened, the new house would not be burned down. He had previously given it as his opinion that the burnings which had occurred near Sneem during the 'troubled times' were due to bad organisation. In the district which he ran at Carragh Lake during the same period, no burnings had taken place. Mr Palmer, the school teacher backed him up, saying that they had been altogether a mistake.

More than a decade had passed since the Troubles, but old passions continued. Several people standing near the table, who, it seemed, had taken an active part in the said burnings, began to murmur and raise their fists. Things cooled down and no blows were exchanged, perhaps because two of the guests were garda. And J.J. was there; afterwards he said to my father, 'I quelled them with a look.' More speeches assured us that the new house would never be destroyed by fire intentionally.

The boatloads dispersed by moonlight. Nanny Somers rounded us up at last and put us to bed in one of the little cabins in the new house. Lying one on top of the other in the ship's bunks, through the window we could hear a chorus of 'For He's a Jolly Good Fellow' as men and women marched or stumbled to the waiting boats. Of the forty-two dozen bottles of beer about twenty remained. No one drowned, although a fair share of the guests fell into the tide on the way home. In the words of J.J. they had the sea salt on their lips.

6

The Dare Devil Cave

M Y FATHER was determined that much of our food would come from the sea. In those days there were plenty of fish of every variety. Hake, cod and bream, gurnet, together with the unwanted dog fish and shark, were caught in abundance using the technique known as bottom fishing on long lines; dabs and plaice were gathered from the sandy bottom in the net. The lobsters queued to get at the bait in the pots. In August the mackerel were so thick that we were told if you fell into the water you would float on the back of them.

We would go out in rowing boats, dipping feathers in among the shoals that pattered on the sea's surface and bringing up six at a time. We felt the exhilaration of success about those daily expeditions, filling up the gunwale with fish – far too many ever to eat, too many to offer to the inhabitants of Sneem and round about.

Only a few years before, the coastal ports would have been filled with girls coming down from Donegal to gut the striped fish and pickle it in barrels for the American market. But now the Americans did not want Irish mackerel, nor did the Irish want to eat them. Nor did the gentry. Mackerel, as Edith Somerville once observed, was not company fish. Nor was herring, whose shoals were caught by local people in biblical quantities during the winter months, and often dumped and left to rot because even after the poor had paid pennies for their fill, there was no transport to take the rest to market. Not for nothing were Friday meals penitential.

In the sea around us you could get quantities of fish with long lines and short lines and spinners. There was the 'puzzle net' for catching mullet. The net floated on the surface and the mullet would be trapped below floating seaweed. When we were older we went on expeditions to catch herring by night, travelling with torches in the motor boat through the narrow length of Garnish Sound, which was only a little wider than the boat. The net would be set in the evening during the transient period between twilight and dark. Then we would return when it was fully dark and pick the fish out by torchlight by hand – the mackerel caught securely in the tangles of the net, the herring swimming in until the net bulged. All around the island small boats could be seen bobbing around the estuaries and bays filled with other fishermen.

In late summer we would watch the mackerel themselves turn hunters and go after whitebait. We would sail or row to the nearest strand, where, to the sound of screaming seagulls, shoals of sprat were swirling and rushing towards the shore and away in fright. Their predators waited for them. Sooner or later a good many of those little fish would end up in mackerels' stomachs, or else they would be driven to despair and would cast themselves up on the beach. The next day the shore would have an edge more silver and lacy than foam – a hemline of a million dead sprats. Behind them the blue surface of the sea heaved as the mackerel, striped like tigers, manoeuvred, hesitated, and then all together in a pack lunged at the terrified little fishes driven like buffalo before Indians.

We would fill buckets with whitebait, the easiest and basest sort of help-yourself fishing. The catch would be given to Cook to prepare, sweating and red-faced in the little kitchen off the sitting room. She filled a brown paper bag with flour, and put a handful of fish in before she shook it. Then they were deep fried and served with brown vinegar spilled out of the bottle, better than crisps, the only kind of fish we really liked.

But other fish had to be eaten, mackerel mostly, at least a fraction of what had been caught, scored and laid in roasting pans a greasy dozen at a time. Huge bland pollock, which always tasted of tissue paper and pins. Every other fish was fried. Blue smoke filtered everywhere and the little house reeked with fishy smells like an old trawler.

'Fishing was excellent . . . doubt if any of us had eaten so much before,' my father would record. And the next day there would be another expedition. No one declared that they had had enough. There were even too many lobsters. In the waters off the island pots were laid each morning and any amount came to take the bait. It was a poor day when the pots came up empty. Usually several were tortured to death and served up scarlet on lettuce, accompanied by freshly dug new potatoes. We had endless debates about whether lobsters screamed. Better to flee the kitchen before the water boiled.

Lobsters might suffer, but fish could not be left to writhe and gasp before they died. My father would become impatient. Boys had to learn early on the rapid form of butchery that required detaching six mackerel from wicked hooks and smartly breaking their necks.

There was so much to kill. Over the years the annual

consignment of half a dozen hens brought down from Dublin in the van was supposed to provide the company with fresh eggs, but lay as they might, the poor birds could never produce enough, so that they ended up in the pot. Together with my mother, whose love of wild creatures was selective, we would watch Jerry, a wild looking figure with an axe, chasing the startled hens into bushes; first caught, first beheaded. It was shocking to observe that a headless hen really did walk about for a few seconds afterwards. The traumatised remainder would take to trees.

Mullet were muddy fish with little prissy mouths that would not take bait and had to be netted or shot. The Mullet King, a tall man with a skull-like face who lived on the far side of the Kenmare River, frightened us with his stories. He would not bathe for fear of being bitten by a conger eel. He had seen a girl who was bathing come out of the sea, and she was followed by a conger onto the grass. He himself had been chased over the fields by a gigantic conger, even larger. 'She had the head on her the size of a young calf with teeth which would crush a man if he was caught.'

The Mullet King was all skin and bone which may have been why he was spared. He told us how the congers came from the hairs of cows' and horses' tails, and that even if the hairs were tied into twenty knots, they would still separate and turn into eels. He showed us the place where the congers came to die; he had come across the biggest yet, lying on the shore.

Congers lived among the rocks just under the place where we swam.

'Nonsense, they won't touch you,' Phil insisted.

'How do you know?'

'They have quite enough to eat in the sea without bothering us.'

One thrilling summer evening we went with my father and his friends in the *Memphis* on our first conger safari. Special bait had to be prepared; sheep's guts from the butcher in Sneem were the essential delicacy to entice them from their hidden caves. The large baited hooks were fastened to wire rather than rope so that the monsters could not bite through them.

The best time for conger fishing was at dusk and low tide. The long pier at Garnish or the pier at the Parknasilla Hotel were reputed to have the largest and most fearsome eels. We rowed out to Garnish where four men in black mackintoshes and two small boys leaned out of the boat and lowered steel-protected lines into the water which was lit with phosphorescence created by the plankton that ruled the night sea.

'There!' Down through the bright water we could make out a conger like an enormous electrically lit sea serpent.

'There's another!'

I dangled my line nervously. 'When it bites, give your line a sharp tug!' Not mine, I prayed, and my prayer was answered. From the stern came the yell, 'I've got one!'

'Hold the line!'

'For God's sake, don't rock the boat!'

A huge wriggling black shape was pulled aboard and was lashing about on the floor. Four grown men and two excited boys took twenty minutes to kill it. A conger has twice as many lives as a cat.

We took it back and hung it on a line to dry. Even the dogs turned away from conger steak. It was a trophy like a dead tiger, grey above and white below, its dorsal fin running down its back, with large eyes that were disconcertingly intelligent.

'Only medium size, I'm afraid,' said my father.

There were optional forms of slaughter. Cousin Ralph (a commander for a change, not a colonel) who had a property above Sneem, had access to thousand acres of shooting, mostly vertical. This sort of killing in the bleak Kerry mountains was not for small boys, only for my father and his friends. He took part in shoots reluctantly, since dispatching birds meant a day off from the blood sports he preferred. But his guests liked a change from killing mackerel, and he went along.

We started off at 10 a.m. on a hot day to climb the mountains to the west of the Sneem valley. It got hotter and the going was difficult. On and on we trudged without sight of anything . . . We had ceased to hope – suddenly from just in front of us four grouse got up – not a shot was fired. I had a hammer gun, and of course was not ready . . . As we regained the cars, exhausted, one of the dogs, a setter, threw a fit on the ground. I confess it seemed a fitting gesture. They got the poor dog going again by rubbing it hard with fresh wet moss chiefly in the face . . .

Cormorant-shooting was more enjoyable, 'a most pleasant pastime', wrote my father.

At first it was thought the best practice was to shoot wildly enough to keep the bird under waters so that it becomes exhausted and gives time for a steady aim, but it was found that for one bird, when it was tired, a hundred rounds were used before it was finally hit. It was thus considered too extravagant and more accurate shooting was used with great success.

It was hard to understand why my father permitted hare hunts on the island, but I suppose he wanted to protect the thousands of trees he had planted. Groups of men would come over with their dogs and chase the unfortunate hares to the end of the island where they were killed. Very soon none were left. In the local community the hare hunt was regarded as a fine legitimate sport, and even today coursing has its defenders.

Better to stick to sailing or to the development of the island. Belinda, the handsome black Dexter cow who provided us with a particularly rich milk, was part of my father's drive for self-sufficiency. Belinda's constant companion was Dinah the donkey who worked for her living pulling a little cart around the island. Both animals had been ferried over from the Oysterbed. Dinah's tasks were endless, from carrying seaweed up from the rocks to be used to manure the vegetables, to bringing up the loads of coral which had been collected on the coral strand west of us, from the harbour to where they were laid on the paths. Belinda and Dinah were inseparable. When Belinda was milked by Jerry or Denis the donkey would gravely watch the proceedings, and when Dinah was harnessed for carrying her baskets of seaweed, or was performing her other duties, the cow would always be walking behind her.

My father's friends continued to be put to work, clearing land or painting boats and after their exertions they would be rewarded by relaxing in the newly built house. The views from the windows of the sitting room compensated for any sense of claustrophobia. Charts, maps, telescopes covered the walls, yachting manuals took up most of the book shelf, apart from some old Penguin detective stories. A ship's drink

locker from an old clipper ship held bottles tightly in place.
On rainy days a dozen or so guests assembled there, and from
early morning the scent of the turf fire filled the room.

'This is a list of those who stayed with Joyce and self
during the summer of 1935 in order of their appearance,' my
father wrote. There were more than twenty.

Who were the people who made up my father's court?
My two uncles came down occasionally with their wives,
who were not at all keen on the discomfort they were
offered. Aunt Grace always remembered the moment when
scalding tea went down the back of her neck as Bernadette
passed the teapot through the hatch from the kitchen.

One of my father's best friends was Harry Michael, a GP
from Malahide, who got to love Kerry so much that he
acquired a Nissen hut beside the Oysterbed Pier which was
nearly as uncomfortable as the house on the island. There
was Tom Harmon who motored over regularly from County
Cork and Colonel Fitzsimon and Mabel who lived in a
Dublin suburb not far from Farmhill. Fitz had an interesting
past. When he was in the army after the First World War, he
had to do all the arrangements about finding a really anony-
mous body which would become the Unknown Soldier and
then he had to get the eternal flame at Westminster Abbey
into place.

There were West Cork cousins from Castletownshend
who were nearly as fanatical about sailing as my father was.
There were the foreigners, the Swedish and German doctors,
who shared with my father his passionate interest in the
treatment of TB. There were the odd neighbours, who came
over for the day and returned to their damp houses which
they suddenly found quite comfortable. There were quite a

lot of women, friends of my mother and medical colleagues of my father.

It was hard to know whom my father admired. A brilliant surgeon or successful general was not immune from criticism. 'Freddy suffered from the complaint of not being able to prevent the boat from going about whenever it wanted to, and Patrick holds the time record for sailing when still attached to the mooring.'

Every morning guests would climb out of their narrow bunks to make their way to one of the Elsans, inside or out, or to take a shower. There was no bath in the island house. 'Don't waste the water!' someone would shout after a minute. Water was strictly rationed since it had to be pumped manually from the ground floor cistern to a smaller tank on the roof, and then come down again through tap and shower head. Every morning brought the slow rhythm of the pump back and forwards by Jimmy or Jerry who rowed over from the mainland. In addition to Cook and a succession of maids, during our early years, Nanny Somers, Jerry and Jimmy performed vital tasks. They milked the cow, cleaned the paths, gardened under my mother's direction, emptied out the Elsan and killed the hens.

In the little hall my father placed a Victorian letter box with a brass plate marked LETTERS. Every day from Sneem four miles away came the burly figure of Jimmy the post, riding his ancient bicycle through fuchsia lanes or the clotted tropical vegetation of Reenafera. When he reached the rock nearest to us he would remove his heavy serge jacket and leather boots and let out a long melancholy whistle. We would row over and find him smoking his pipe, his feet dangling in the water.

'Not a bad day, thank God,' he would say, taking and handing over letters and accepting our gift of mackerel, which he would tie to the bars of the bike. 'Another grand day for fishing. But she's going to change.'

'She' controlled the rain, wind and sun. 'She's looking good.' 'She's looking bad.' 'She's after giving me the fool's race.'

Some days there would be four short whistles, a pause and then a longer whistle. This meant a telegram, usually a message to annoy.

'Car broken down. Stop. Have you any means of rescuing me?'

My father would say as he went down to the boathouse, 'I can see no point in wasting a day taken away from fishing or sailing.'

Guests had to make their own arrangements. If they were held up by a flock of black-faced sheep or their cars failed them, they were expected to find their own way to the Oysterbed Pier. Even then someone would be dispatched with the greatest reluctance to fish them out. Only when a visitor actually drove his car off the pier was a full scale rescue operation mounted. Luckily it was low tide.

'Idiot,' said my father as the luckless man was hauled to safety. 'Next time he won't be stopping in any of those Killarney pubs.'

Another victim of the Oysterbed was Miss Brand who came down to the island with Marjorie and Arthur Chance, and their young protégé, Noel Browne, later a controversial politician of whom my father would greatly disapprove. They arrived by moonlight, and while rapturously admiring the sea and the dark coastline, Miss Brand fell over the edge. It was low springtide and the drop was about twenty feet. She landed on some rocks and bounced into the sea. They hauled her out unscathed, and she gratefully drank quantities of brandy which a camper on the pier gave them. They drove on to the Parknasilla Hotel, and got through a fair amount of whiskey. In the small hours Con, the Parknasilla boatman, brought them out to the island and the household was roused.

'Fool!' my father said, but my mother took pity on the still-shaken girl and gave her some gin. She recovered enough next day to go out sailing.

On Sundays family and guests were hauled off to church. Earlier Cook and the maids had been rowed over to the mainland, and gone off on foot to Mass, making the perilous journey through Reenafera, avoiding the snarls of Nicky the Alsatian that belonged to Colonel Knowles. Jerry would row them back in time to prepare our lunch. An hour or so later it was the turn of the Quality.

'Put on decent togs.'

My father would appear in suit and tie, my mother would be wearing a hat and a fox biting its tail round her neck, and all the guests in church-going clothes looked different, as if suddenly church-going was the most important thing in their lives. The sun always seemed to shine brightest on Sundays. We had to tear ourselves away from everything which meant freedom and fun for another dreary service. The *Memphis* had to be hauled into the pier and the dogs ejected. Would the outboard start? Often Phil and I in our Sunday clothes had to take to the oars while the rest of the smart party acted as lookouts for rocks. We moored at the Oysterbed and took cars into Sneem to the small Church of

Ireland church which had a copper salmon turned to green flying over the roof.

Many sunny mornings offering the best of sailing weather and perfect hours for island pursuits were passed ('wasted' in our opinion) in the half empty little church. A few like-minded local families and a proportion of retired army people living in the area would be there to be counted, perhaps displaying the outward and visible sign of an inward and spiritual grace. The numbers of my father's friends swelled the congregation healthily as we sang to the organ which had survived another winter's damp and wheezed away as Miss Beamish banged at it. What did 'Pavillioned in Splendour' mean? It took a gale for my father to relent from the routine. If we were really unlucky, more time would be wasted when morning service was followed by an invitation to sherry and G and T at the home of one of the colonels.

At the western end of the island was an area we called Cowland, which was left in its original wild state. The screes of rock were covered with seaweed which flapped over inlets and rock pools facing the open sea and beyond in the distance the lines of mountains on the other side of the Kenmare River. The pools were filled with shrimps, crabs and anemones the colour of blood, either curled up like buttons or with their tendrils waving in the tidal water as they looked for their lunch. Further out in the deep water were sea urchins, who protected themselves from the sun by making little hats out of shells which they stuck to their spines.

On the edge of Cowland Phil and I found a small cave and facing it a grey stone cliff as smooth as glass.

'You climb first!'

'No, you do!'

'Coward!'

Phil made the first attempt to go up. When you looked carefully you could make out minute cracks etched along the surface, just enough for a precarious toe hole. He went up a few yards and then stuck, unable to go up or down. He had to let go and slid down, cutting open his knee and leg.

'I told you not to wander around without telling anyone!' My mother dabbed away with cotton wool, unusually annoyed.

'It was just bad luck.'

'You might have broken your leg.'

We were gated for a couple of days, missing a boating party and a picnic on another island. While everyone was away we went down to the rock and tried again.

'It's easy,' Phil said. 'All you have to do is to take off your shoes.'

'You fell . . .' I pointed to his leg which was still stained with petunia-coloured mecurochrome to kill the germs.

'Don't be so stupid. There are plenty of cracks for fingers and toes.' He set off again, taking a more diagonal line. I followed, trying not to look down.

'There's a crack over your right arm.'

'I can't see!'

'Hold on.'

Phil was on top. 'You need to learn a correct sense of balance.'

A last desperate heave and I, too, was sitting beside my brother in a couch of grass and heather; below us was the little cave, a stony beach, and in the distance some rocks on which lay a family of seals, the babies woolly and white, the adults mottled like slugs.

We broke the news of the cave and the rock to my parents. My mother did not like it at all. 'They might really hurt themselves climbing the rock.'

But my father, who had the power, let us continue with our plans. 'It's time they learned some initiative.'

'And what happens if the roof of the cave falls in?'

'It's perfectly safe. I'm far more worried they'll do something really asinine like swimming out too far.'

We were given a couple of broken chairs and a large sea chest with knives, forks, cups and spoons; a tattered piece of sailcloth covered the floor of the cave. A hurricane lamp with a candle and some saucepans completed our independence.

In those early years of island life our Dare Devil Cave became our second home, far enough away from the main house where our parents and their friends could intimidate us. A wriggling coral path led to one of the island's deep valleys filled with newly planted tree ferns. Then the valley burst into the open and I can remember the pleasure in getting away from the grown-ups and being surrounded on three sides by open sea. Far away to the right danced the Kerry mountains. On a summer's day mountains, sea and scattered islands shimmered in the sun.

In front of us were rock pools and a small beach, all our own. At low tide we could search for shells, and after a storm there was the excitement of finding a glass fisherman's float washed up, a sea green or clear glass bubble. The Lookout Rock stood just outside the cave, covered with a cushion of pinks on which we could lie looking out to sea.

In the early years from our lookout we might catch a sight of the old sailing trawler, the *Maria Long*, which used to sail down to Parknasilla on most days to sell fish. But the day came when she sank off Sherkey, and the trawler master, his mate and his dog nearly drowned. 'Thrilling Story of a Pom's Rescue' was headlined in the *Examiner*. 'Trawler master's love nearly proves fatal.'

Captain O'Mahoney, who had survived being torpedoed during the First World War, was interviewed.

I looked into my little cabin and saw water about three feet down there. I shouted, 'O'Connor get into the dinghy, look after the oars. I must get our little Pom.' I felt the *Maria* fast sinking under me. I had my little dog under my arm and jumped into the dinghy. The water was nearly over the *Maria* at the time, and I cannot say where I got the knife that cut the painter when the boat sank, carrying all our gear and belongings with her.

The gear included the mainsail and jib belonging to one of my father's yachts which he was repairing at the time.

Inside our cave we learned the joys of cooking as sausages were blackened over a small open fire and eaten with mugs of tea. Toast, biscuits and cakes were kept in a tin, while shrimps caught in the rock pools were boiled. The small necessities of life were there in the cave and, as we grew, the rock got easier to climb. We could watch the seals, look for lines of porpoises out to sea turning their glistening backs in the sun, and once or twice glimpsed an otter which had come over from the mainland streaking across the heavy red seaweed.

Phil had to make things more complicated. 'We'll have a club. The Dare Devil Club. Only people who can climb the rock can join.'

We had the perfect candidates, the Knowles boys from

Reenafera across the water. The Knowles boys, who were around the same age as us, were already destined to go to Sandhurst and follow their father into the British army. A lot of our friends were like that. Meanwhile we knew they wouldn't shirk the Dare Devil test.

'That doesn't look too difficult.' Robert expertly appraised the climb. 'Shall I go straight up or traverse?'

'Straight up!'

We watched him claw his way to the top where he lit a cigarette. His brother, Peter, followed him. Back in the cave we cut open our wrists and exchanged blood. We lit candles as dusk came and fried bacon and sausages which we ate accompanied by a bottle of cider which the Knowles had smuggled over. Outside there was the sound of waves and the last glimmer of light on the western horizon.

It was a mistake to tell my father about the club as he immediately saw the excuse for a party. To celebrate he gave us a small punt which we christened *Sudden Death* with a bottle of fizzy lemonade. Phil painted a skull and crossbones on the sail and, watched by friends and relatives, we set out from the pier. The name proved too apt.

'Keep bailing!'

'Pull at the oars! Watch out for rocks!'

'Someone go and rescue them,' my mother said.

My father said, 'If they insist on sitting together in the stern, no wonder the punt is sinking.'

A painter was thrown and the single sail with its skull and crossbones collapsed around our heads.

It was never easy to be entirely independent. My father found time to watch our development closely. 'Peter managed to swim. Phil did the trick. He went into Sneem and bought him an air ring. This gave Peter confidence and after using it two or three times he threw it away and never used it again.'

Swimming was easier than messing about in boats under my father's critical eye. 'Both the boys improved greatly at rowing but so far neither has much idea of sailing.'

We were very young when he acquired two twelve-foot dinghies for us. Romantically called the *Gypsy* and the *Lady Ann*, they were the size of those boats sailed with such infuriating competence by the children in Arthur Ransome's books.

My father watched us tacking, gybing and going about. He expected us to tie the correct knot, know the difference between port and starboard, how to handle long lines and the correct anchor drill. Phil soon learned. How could two brothers be so different? When I clutched slippery rope, the simplest knot became a granny. The *Gypsy* floundered under my command as I tried to manoeuvre around the creeks and rocks to angry sounds heard in the distance. Sometimes I would hear him from the shore where he stood and shouted. Or, together with a crew of his friends whom I believed were constantly jeering at me, he followed me in the *Puffin*, bellowing commands and advice.

'Keep your head into the wind.'

Herons flew ahead of me with their heavy beat and seals slipped off rocks rather than stay and watch me perform under his disapproving gaze. His voice carried over the water.

'Look out, she's gybing!'

The granny knot holding up the mainsail slipped and the sail smothered me as it fell and the boom swayed in the wind.

'Next time don't take Bruin with you!'

I hadn't wanted Bruin, but he was a true sea dog and had developed the habit of leaping into the *Gypsy* and installing himself as passenger. Once he was on board, he was too heavy for me to throw out. Bruin preferred the *Gypsy* to the *Lady Ann* which Phil was tacking neatly towards Garnish Island. Slimy and steaming, his tongue hanging out in ecstasy, he sat in the bows, and at the command of 'About!' either refused to move or made a jump into the water. Should I gybe and try and pick him up? I could never pull him back into the rocking boat. The wind was rising. Should I leave him and hope my father would pick him up in the *Puffin*? Should I try and get out of earshot?

'Go about – no, not like that – you'll capsize if you gybe like that.'

'Bring her up. You're running onto a lee shore!'

He persisted, giving me his time when he would have preferred doing other things, and later I was grateful to him. He may have used the tactics of a bully, and I could have done without his friends, the gallery of spectators, who must have got bored watching a small boy floundering in a wavering boat drifting into difficulties until it had to be rescued. But, thanks to him, I finally learned to steer and sail and follow Phil. And he let us go off on our own. Our world opened up to the blue waters of the Kenmare River and its surroundings. The two small dinghies with their bright red sails could penetrate into the most hidden and secret places.

7

Laragh

SOON AFTER THE great inaugural party on Illaunslea my father decided that running a surgeon's practice, over-seeing Farmhill and developing his island property in Kerry did not take up enough of his time. With the country in the depths of the economic war and depression, he sought a new expensive challenge. He bought a large country estate not too far from Dublin in County Wicklow.

Laragh House had numerous rooms, together with all sorts of dark holes which were called offices. Outside were yards and outhouses, and half a dozen cottages and gate lodges scattered over eight hundred acres. The place was totally run down. The house had been empty for years and damp and decay had got to it, while the hilly land was untilled and a great part of the woods had been cut down.

A previous owner had been connected by marriage to the Bartons and Childers associated with Glendalough House, who had played their considerable part in recent Irish history. But Mr Booth did not appear to have been interested in patriotism or politics. We were told that he had hanged himself from the chandelier in the main hall after sustaining gambling debts in Monte Carlo.

We were full of excitement when my mother took us to see Laragh for the first time. We drove out from Dublin in her Ford, slowly up into the Wicklow Hills beyond Bray, across Calary bog, through Roundwood, past Derrylossery, past the mill where the infant Laurence Sterne had fallen in and nearly drowned, and down towards Glendalough. We approached the little hamlet of Annamoe; if you blinked, you missed it. Although it was midsummer, we drove into mist and rain and were greeted for the first time by Laragh's perpetual air of autumn. In future years we would learn how the dank grey clouds had a special potency. It was a coincidence that my father chose two of the wettest places in Ireland to live in. Like Kerry, County Wicklow, the Garden of Ireland, had a surfeit of rain.

A little past Annamoe we came to a ruined gate lodge and a mile-long avenue full of potholes darkened by rhododendrons. After a time we caught sight of a house which was covered with ivy and shaded by laurels. A little black lake with three small islands lay beside it.

On the lawn in front of the porch grew two great Wellingtonias whose long tapering branches swept down to the ground, and reached to the sky.

'Race you to the top!'

'No! No!'

We ignored our mother's cries which grew fainter as we tackled the sticky resin-coated branches. Soon I was treading air, looking down on the grey roof of the house and gardens and the two yards, one with the bell tower from which a bell summoned the men to work. Below me was a walled garden and sloping fields which reached towards the Wicklow Hills, some sitka forest and a stretch of bog belonging to the place, over which we had turbary rights.

I could see Laragh and Annamoe, fronted by Trooperstown

Hill, and beyond were waves of mountains concealing Glendalough with its churches and round tower, and further villages with the lovely names of Wicklow, Tinahely, Rathdrum and Aughrim. Phil was waving to me as he swayed at the tapered top of the other tree, and a hundred feet below I could make out the minute figure of my mother surrounded by the pieces of fluff which were the dogs.

We came down at last, and were introduced to the house. The rooms smelt of damp and mould, and some buckets had been placed along the corridors under the leaking roof. There were numerous bedrooms served by a couple of bathrooms whose baths were streaked in green. We inspected the drawing room and billiard room, the peeling walls of the servant quarters and the kitchen which led into larders and sculleries. Across the yard, whose cobbles shone with rain, we explored endless lopsided outbuildings. Altogether just the place for my father.

In the hall the chandelier was still there.

'Do you think he broke the news of all the money he had lost to his family before he killed himself?'

'How do you know he had a family?'

'Perhaps he had a mistress.'

The idea of the old landlord spinning like a top would be the subject of endless debate and nightmare. How did he get up that far to tie the rope? A chair would not have been high enough. Did he use a stepladder? How long was he dangling before they cut him down? The house would always be full of people, but plenty of unexplained noises could be interpreted as footsteps. Would he still be wearing his rope collar?

We never saw Mr Booth's ghost, although we kept a permanent lookout for it. Perhaps the melancholy we felt in

Laragh during the years ahead emanated from his presence. More likely he fled away as my father began to carry out his grandiose ideas.

My father would not have touched the place if it had been habitable or smart in any way. Here was another enterprise he could start from scratch, a rundown estate which offered a splendid challenge. It would be turned into a luxurious country house hotel. He was not deterred by the fact that he was entirely lacking in business experience and knowledge of hotel management.

Uncle Bris had died by this time and there was more money with which to play ducks and drakes. The dividends of the National Railways of Mexico and Brazil, the Rumanian Consolidated Loan, Travancore Tea Estates, South African Breweries and many more financed my father's schemes. At least he did not go to Monte Carlo like Mr Booth.

We continued to live at Farmhill while the transformation took place. Occasionally we were brought down to admire the mended roof, the new 'Rose Annex', the new bedrooms smelling of paint, built in a corner of the lower yard, the Directors' Room and the cocktail bar. The impressive new ballroom with a maple floor was designed by Michael Scott.

Laragh House would be a proper country house hotel catering for every country sport in the book. A dozen new stables were built and a riding field was laid out with jumps. Two hard courts offered tennis in all weathers, and soon guests would be batting balls at each other in drizzle. The smooth croquet lawn provided something less strenuous for the elderly whose partners could hold umbrellas over them as they aimed at the hoops. The lake would be used as a swimming pool.

A laundry house would cater for the guests' sheets and towels; the wood mill would take care of fuel, and the battery house was necessary for the turbine which would provided electricity.

The most extravagant enterprise was the construction of not one but two golf courses, a full eighteen-hole course, and a nine-hole for softies. My father had the greatest contempt for people who liked golf, but he realised that such a Philistine pastime would have to be catered for at a sports hotel. Fir trees were felled and greens and bunkers scattered around with the aid of many more workers than had civilised the island, all toiling like Pharaoh's slaves without a bulldozer in sight. All the levelling and planting that had been done on the island seemed a small effort by comparison.

The whole enterprise, hotel and farm with its hundreds of acres, would be run by my mother, who at last would be able to have her own horses. This fact alone made her agree to all my father's ideas. We entered into her plans; she pictured us achieving numerous triumphs at the Horse Show, or at least becoming fearless huntsmen.

The name Philip means lover of horses and at least Phil had a good seat and light hands. But I lacked any similar talent, as I lacked the skill to be a competent sailor. I had been an equestrian failure from the time I was placed on a donkey at the age of four. Humiliation came soon afterwards at the annual Farmhill fête which was attended by the popular Lord Mayor of Dublin, Alfie Byrne, wearing his gold chain with the medallion showing King Billie. I was on the back of an animal named Amber who bolted, after being frightened by the crowd, and threw me. While my mother's attention was taken up by the donkey – when she said 'poor little fellow' she did not mean me – muddy and yelling, I was comforted by one of the ladies behind the tea urn who gave me a cake, and the Lord Mayor came over to ask how the little lad was.

'I hate donkeys,' I screamed.

'So do I!' Alphie Byrne agreed. He was the best Lord Mayor Dublin ever had.

My mother persevered and kitted us out with jodhpurs, hacking jackets, riding boots and black bowlers. She sent us to Colonel Hume Dudgeon who had run the equitation centre at Sandhurst, and had now retired to Dublin to found a famous riding school. Charming and always immaculately turned out, with a flower in his buttonhole, the Colonel would supervise supercilious young men who had been sent over from smart English cavalry regiments to brush up their riding skills. In those days everyone in the cavalry still had to learn to ride and it took the Second World War to put an end to that sort of thing. As they hung around the stables smoking cigarettes those young officers exuded an air of nonchalance and privilege.

Children were left to the mercies of the Colonel's colleague, Sergeant Major MacMaster, whose voice, no doubt, had terrified plenty of troops. Perhaps his bark was worse than his bite.

'If I catch any of you miserable creatures mistreating your pony I promise you'll never ride again.'

Fat little girls with pudgy faces and nervous small boys rode in a circle earnestly trying to impress the Sergeant

Major that we were not going to stick pins into our ponies' rumps.

'While I'm here you bloody well learn to respect your animals.'

Riding lessons were dominated by his bellowing and his swagger stick poking into the small of our backs. 'Sit up straight, not like that – you look like a bloody question mark. Don't slouch . . . knees in. I can see a view of Ticknock between you and the saddle, Mister Peter. That poor bloody animal has stopped and is gazing at the ground because he is depressed – do you hear me? How can you expect the horse to obey you if you don't give him any lead?'

It was usually Peter who was selected for the ten shilling note ordeal. The money placed between calf and saddle – 'If you can hang onto it the whole way round you can keep it' – always fluttered down to the sawdust.

'What sort of bloody rider do you think you are? It'll be a good few thousand years before you are ready for the bleeding Grand National!'

Meanwhile we were being prepared for boarding school. It was decided that Phil and I would go to different schools. Phil's abilities had overshadowed me, and perhaps I would thrive away from him.

Schools in Ireland attended by little Protestant boys faithfully adhered to the austere tradition of English scholastic establishments with an extra element of lunacy all their own. A system that allowed any pervert or retired army officer to buy a preparatory school rather than a chicken farm was asking for trouble.

Our uniforms were bought in Switzers, the great department store in Grafton Street whose lofty halls rang with the sounds of money whizzing up in little tubes to the high control desk where a girl sat and unfastened them and sent them down again with change.

'Baymount and Castle Park,' my mother said to the elderly assistant and lists were produced. Blazers, two herringbone jackets, two grey Vyella shirts, pyjamas, ties, stockings, belts with snake buckles, Oxford brown lace-up shoes and Billy Bunter hats. Mine had the initials BS for Baymount School, Phil's CP for Castle Park. The uniforms were identical, except for the colours – puce for Castle Park and striped grey and black for Baymount.

'Go along and see that they fit.'

My mother waited beside the polished counter with the brass measuring ruler made out in inches and yards inserted into the mahogany. Switzers was one of the many shops where she had an account. Brown Thomas, Switzers, Findlaters in Dundrum, O'Brien Corkery in Kenmare, the Swastika laundry and many others received her patronage without actual cash. All her life she kept up an account in Harrods, even though she had bought nothing there since 1932. Like the queen, she did not need to carry money.

Elsewhere in Switzers was the special counter where name tapes were ordered in any colour or font. We were discouraged from choosing green or blue italics and were steered towards plain black Bookman. Since Nanny had departed, it was my mother who had to spend her time sewing into every sock, behind every tie, across beneath every shirt collar. The task took her days, even though our pretentious name was shortened. We were both P.S.Large. Serve her right.

In the schools we were about to attend about 10 per cent of unhappy boys would have double-barrelled names. Some of them would be lords. Meanwhile, we waited in dread, because we knew instinctively that we would be unhappy. Never trust a boy or man who likes or liked his school.

Perhaps my father's conscience was pricked and he remembered some aspect of unhappiness from his past. The day before our departure he recalled a necessity of boarding school life.

'Shouldn't the boys be given some tuck?'

We knew about tuck from reading *Tiger Tim*, but we did not yet recognise the significance of cakes, chocolate and sweets, and perhaps in the early days of term some sausages. As we grew older and wiser we would become aware of the importance of stocking up if we were to survive hardship and not actually starve. There would be many moments of stealing into the darkened tuck room and sitting by a precious box nibbling away. There would be the bullies who would sneak in behind us and demand Danegeld in the form of a piece of chocolate or a slice of cake.

So the last day before the beginning of term was spent in buying small square wooden boxes, together with trips to Findlaters for some solid fruitcake, and the sweet shop for sweets and chocolates that would provide extra rations. In our nursery, two trunks filled with new clothes were closed and stencilled with our names at the end of our beds, together with the tuck. It never occurred to our parents that the necessity of tuck boxes was an admission that our schools were not feeding us properly.

At breakfast we were given a meal suitable for condemned men. Instead of the usual porridge and toast we were offered the Sunday special – kedgeree, and eggs, bacon and sausages arranged on the sideboard in dishes covered by silver-plated covers and kept heated by burning wicks. These delicacies failed to lift our spirits.

My father had the nerve to say, 'I never enjoyed school myself, but I know you will both make the best of the experience.'

We said goodbye to the maids and Cook. My mother looked for her car keys which she lost every time she went driving; today she found them all too soon. We climbed into her car together with some dogs. By the time all but Bruin were thrown out our herringbone suits were covered in hairs. So we set off on that rite of passage which was, and for all I know still is, more prolonged and terrible than any circumcision ceremony involving white-painted boys.

The two schools to which we were sent, one on the north side of Dublin, the other on the south, were mirror images. Like Llanabba Castle, the prep school in *Vile Bodies*, both Castle Park and Baymount were converted castellated mansions. It is strange how many private schools in these islands were in this Gothic Revival style, presumably acquired at cheap prices from impoverished gentlemen early this century.

Phil was dropped off at Castle Park, or CP, as he was already calling it. We drove through the high porticoed Gothic gateway down the long avenue to the fortified building. Small boys in their herringbone suits with puce ties and caps were punching each other. A matron dressed in white supervised the unloading of Phil's trunk and tuck box.

Across Dublin Bay a mist floated in from the direction of Howth, as my mother drove me towards the Liffey and over and out to Clontarf, the exact distance away on the north side. The entrance to Baymount was identical to Castle Park,

Uncle Bris painted in Japan, early 1880s.

Uncle Bris, Uncle Phil and my grandfather – Farmhill 1928.

The *Vindex*. Family outing circa 1900.

Crew of the *Vindex*.

Phil and Peter with Bruin, 1932.

The Silver Stream, now in Killarney Motor Museum.

My father and mother with Skelter outside the island house, 1934.

Island house in the early days. The trees had just been planted.

Shira.

Peter on *Shira*, 1938.

Sudden Death being rigged.

Sailing away.

Boating, 1938.

My mother, Dinny and Bruin.

The Swimming Pool, Laragh House Hotel.

The lake which was always freezing.

Laragh House, spring 1938.

Front of Laragh House Hotel from entrance to Swimming Pool.

My mother, Catherine and
Skelter, 1949.

St Valery, 1949.

the same Gothic gateway painted gun-metal grey and the long avenue leading to a similar penitentiary.

The poet, Richard Murphy, who was at Baymount with me, wrote:

> Describe a gate lodge like a dragon's mouth
> Taking in boys and parents with a grin
> Then spitting out the parents, iron teeth
> Close when the last proud vintage car has gone.

A similar matron, thinner than the one at Castle Park, stood on the steps.

'I am sure you will love it,' my mother repeated as the gravel crunched under the wheels. There was no uncertainty in her voice.

From another car a boy was struggling to remain seated. 'Be brave!' urged a tall woman wearing one of the pixie hats stuck with feathers popular in the 1930s. But he was hollering loudly.

My mother dabbed a kiss in my direction and drove away; I could see Bruin leaning out of the back window of the car sniffing the breeze; lucky, lucky dog.

I do not know if I was more unhappy than most small boys at boarding school, but whenever I go to church I say a prayer for them.

8

A Good Name Is
Worth Millions

MY MOTHER WAS creating a garden on Illaunslea. It would be to her taste, not a green home for dinosaurs, dominated by tree ferns, and tropical plants beloved by the Robinsonians, but a landscape of more delicate vistas with azaleas, annuals, shrubs, all sorts of roses, fruit trees and vegetables.

From early on she took over the responsibility for the planting of trees. Once my father had mapped out the forestation of the island, he concentrated on boats. What was astonishing was how quickly things grew under her direction. In what seemed no time at all the bare vistas of rocks took on the look of a forest. Soon the island was thickly wooded and the garden, tended by Jerry during our absence, took shape.

Year by year she made careful notes of her gardening operations, beginning with twenty-five Nordman silver firs planted in 1932, nearly all of which died. Other failures were recorded. An acre of firs near the bathing place was 'too exposed, many of the trees died'. 'Delayed by post and six died' was the fate of a batch of heaths. Some delphiniums were eaten by slugs and the deodars and cedars of Lebanon perished, together with a plantation of fifty larches. But 'doing well' or 'quite well' or 'very good' were more typical comments in her diary.

I remember the second summer when she brought down two small eucalyptuses in pots; in little more than a decade they were over a hundred feet high. Not only did she supervise the planting of trees, but personally dug the border areas, the roses and the places for shrubs and rock plants. A few blousy purple rhododendrons were trained to form a tunnel leading up to the house from the pier, but otherwise she eschewed the giant rhododendrons which were fashionable. In nearby gardens like Garnish they grew to a hundred feet high with red flowers as big as dinner plates, and there were different species for every month in the year. My mother preferred low-growing azaleas which smelled of honey. Her work was joy. 'I wonder if this little thing might do better on the far side of the rock?'

The orchard flourished; the Worcester pearmains and Irish peach apples planted in 1933 were fruiting two years later. She planted gooseberries, raspberries, a Victoria plum, a Mary Duke cherry and three pear trees. Some things were obtained locally, the fuchsia, bamboo and hydrangeas. Others were taken from rooted cuttings or came from friends.

'I thought you would like these to add to your collection.'

'What a darling!' She would open the soggy bag of plants and *Trachlelium diptercarput* or *Silene pendula compacta* would be added to her garden. But most plants came from nurseries around Dublin – Watsons, Drummonds or Pattons. Soon ericas and lavenders, blue geraniums, honeysuckle and roses of every variety began to grow and spread. Besides the herbaceous plants, the rock plants and shrubs, quick growing annuals were scattered to brighten up late summer days.

Vegetables were laid out in black earth in a valley close to the house. No vegetables ever tasted better; the new potatoes, wiped clean, were like truffles. In one year, 1934, carrots, onions, lettuce, cabbage, peas, French beans, curly kale, parsley, celery and sprouting broccoli were planted. Only the curly kale and the broccoli did not come to harvest. Unfamiliar with them, Jerry dug them up, thinking they had gone wrong.

For most of the time my mother managed to avoid sailing, quoting George Herbert's advice, 'Praise the sea, but stay on land.' I never remember my father lifting a spade. Instead he persisted in his sailing operations, taking his unfortunate friends along with him. Every year his fleet grew larger and the boathouse grew fuller. The eighteen-foot *Puffin* with a centreboard and a Bermuda sail, was soon considered wholly inadequate and was followed by the *Tern*, a three-ton yawl which he sailed down from Scotland in the inevitable storm – his log makes me queasy just to read. Then *Kingfisher*, was acquired, a thirty-foot motor cruiser which, he hoped, would provide an alternative for those who didn't enjoy more rugged sailing. She had luxuries like electric lighting, a saloon that gave full headroom to most people and bunks which were wide and long. He considered it a ladies' boat.

His greatest love was the *Shira*, a large Lough Fyne cutter which he bought from Lord Dunraven in 1936. For this new vessel he acquired a new deckhand to take the place of Dempsey who had sailed in the *Tern* where he had made a habit of washing his feet in buckets of fish. The new man, Brosnan, my father was told by the harbour master at Dingle who recommended him, was far more refined. Unlike Dinny or Jerry, the men who worked on the island, the deckhands, being sailors, were called by their surnames. They had a difficult time, since even in a commodious yacht like the *Shira*, Brosnan's quarters were cramped up in the bow beside the anchor chain. His duties consisted of anything from cooking meals to cleaning the brass and holystoning the deck, as well as pulling all the ropes. Phil and I never liked him for his habit of catching dogfish, cutting off their fins and tails and throwing them back live.

The *Shira* was my father's darling. Once aboard, agonies were forgotten, like a woman forgets childbirth, and he would plan ever more ambitious cruises. He would take out engraved black and white canvas-backed sailing charts made up from the survey by Commandant Wolfe and Lieutenant Church who marked out the Irish coast in 1847 at the height of the famine. These charts were updated, principally with soundings in fathoms dotted all over the sea, but until well into the 1970s they were basically unchanged. The compass points were beautifully drawn with elaborate arrows, while the engraved profiles of towns, harbours and mountains and pictures of beacons were still presented as when they were first published a century before. They were works of art. And the information they provided remained true, the tides and directions: 'Rincolisky Castle touching West Skeam leads through . . .'

With the aid of these charts the *Shira* would claw her way way out to the Skelligs and the Blaskets or through Dursey Sound to Bantry Bay. At Castletown Beare my father would often call in on his half-sister Aunt Alice and her husband, Uncle Billy. They had moved there in 1921 just as the IRA were burning Dunboy Castle; the town had been covered with smoke. Aunt Alice had sent a postcard to the Canon at Farmhill with a black and white panoramic view of the town stamped 'Censored by the IRA'. It says plaintively: 'If only I could find a cook.'

Uncle Billy, who was clergyman in this remote parish, had a background as naval chaplain and used to give local young men recommendations if they wanted to join the Royal Navy. He stopped smartly in 1936 after Admiral Somerville was shot by the IRA over at Castletownshend ostensibly for doing the same thing. Meanwhile he had the duty of taking the Sunday service on one of the two British destroyers which were regularly anchored in the sound beside Bear Island. He would motor out in his own launch, the *Heather*, or be escorted in the destroyer's jolly boat. Then he would stand on the deck in his flowing robes, his first world war medals pinned to his cassock, and take Matins for the benefit of the sailors.

Occasionally we were sent to stay with Aunt Alice and Uncle Billy and their five children who were just about our age. Recently I returned to Beare and found the rectory and the stream which we used to dam. Opposite, the platform for crossroads dancing where we watched people dance on summer evenings is still there, and down in the harbour among the trawlers is the little *Heather*.

The *Shira* would round the Mizen to new adventures. My father and his companions might stop at Crookhaven, the first landfall from America whose harbour had once been full of sailing clippers and was now almost deserted. Situated right at the end of West Cork, he found it 'a most eerie place . . . most villages have some pleasant features about them . . .

but this has none.' Nowadays every summer Crookhaven is choked with tourists.

He noted other beautiful coastal towns in a state of dereliction. Kinsale, in particular, with its beautiful eighteenth-century merchants' houses and old women who still wore the graceful Cork cloak, was a wretched bedraggled place.

He might visit Castletownshend, where Edith Somerville and her relations lived in claustrophobic proximity. Things changed slowly there; I remember tennis parties, late in the 1930s where the players used old-fashioned wooden rackets and the women wore long skirts.

Once the *Shira* sailed to the Fastnet Lighthouse with fresh fruit, eggs and newspapers for the keepers. While the yacht, in charge of Brosnan, stayed in unusually calm water, my father and his friends landed on the rock, the Teardrop of Ireland, and inspected the bronze doors and shutters that kept out the storms which broke completely over the tower, the cots fitted in the circular rooms and the light – 'six incandescent mantels in two tiers of three each and the shutter revolves by clock-work, the weight falling throughout the tube in the centre of the light-house. One wind-up of this weight lasts about forty minutes.'

Every summer another voyage would be planned and, like Nelson, he would prepare for another bout of seasickness. And, like Nelson, he continued to command and keep the affection and respect of his crew and his friends who suffered as much as he did.

In 1937 he decided to venture farther still. The Coronation Regatta at Torbay provided an ideal test for the capabilities of the *Shira*. In good weather a voyage across the Irish Sea to Devon would be considered little more than a

hen's race. But the winds were strong when he set out with
three (willing) companions and Brosnan. The passage from
Kerry to Cornwall took thirty-six hours and for most of the
time he and his crew were sick and unable to eat or sleep. If
they felt like dozing off they had to ignore the hideous noises
like children in pain, from the blocks and rigging, together
with the deep rumble from the keel which appeared at any
moment liable to break off.

Every miserable moment was logged.

10.00 a.m. Beautiful morning . . . calm . . . slight roll. Wind NW.

11.00 Lumpy sea.

12.30 Wind freshening . . . glass dropping . . . horizon hidden
at times.

17.20 Two reefs taken in.

20.00 Bigger sea . . . wind stronger . . . rolling worse.

23.30 Very heavy rolling, hauled down mainsail.

1.00 Heavy shower. Making no headway under jib. An
increased wind and rising sea – darkness and rain.

The crew endured the usual sailor's problem of things
falling.

Every book, chart and pencil, ruler, dividers, in fact everything
that was taken out, fell repeatedly on the floor, and every time
anything was picked up, the feeling of intense sickness and
exhaustion seemed to become more intense, although such an
increase in misery could hardly have seemed possible.

Later my father summed up the voyage:

Rolling, pitching and twisting, impossible to stand without holding on, impossible to sit except to windward. One man was thrown out of his bunk and hit the one on the other side of the cabin before standing on the floor . . . An hour at the wheel seemed an eternity, time stood still . . . Supposing that the ship rolled once every five seconds, i.e. 720 times an hour, or 25,920 rolls in the complete crossing. But that does not sound enough . . . One could not understand why the ship did not sink when no one much cared whether it did or not.

He went through his usual resolve.

I have lost all shame. I have decided. Never again shall I face the open sea in a small boat – unless the next port can reasonably be expected within 24 hours. That is enough. I am a ditch crawler, a fair-weather sailor, a harbour to harbour man, a coastal creeper – call me what you will, I will not be insulted. That I have come to this resolution does not in an way prevent me from admiring the Ocean Racers and the small boat cruisers. These men are my heroes. I regard them as supermen with veneration – for I have tried and failed. It may be true that an army marches on its stomach, but it is more true that a sailor sails on his, and to put it simply: my stomach won't be sailed on.

But there was plenty more sailing to come, and as the years went by we went along too.

'Peter, do remember to go to the starboard side when you are going to be sick. We can't have you dirtying the decks. Brosnan has enough to do.'

In those days there were few other Irish-based yachts in our vicinity. When the occasional yacht from Cork, or further round the Irish coast, Dun Laoghaire or Howth or the odd stranger who had sailed over from Plymouth or Falmouth, made its way round the Mizen and through the Dursey Sound into the Kenmare River and anchored near Garnish, it was always an occasion. We would row out from the island bringing the crew supplies of fruit and vegetables and later they would join us for a drink and a meal.

Those who called in included Mr Phillpots, a Dublin brewer who had travelled around the Irish coast in a flimsy canvas boat he had made for five pounds. Later, in his workshop in Dublin he showed me a pair of large canvas shoes which he said allowed him to walk on water like Jesus; he intended to walk across Kingstown harbour. He invited me to join him in some sailing expedition, but having seen the boat and heard about the shoes, my father forbade me, and I was glad to obey him.

Conor O'Brien and his tough sister sailed in on the *Saoirse* which he had taken round the world, something of an achievement in those days. The *Saoirse* seemed crude and uncomfortable, and it must have taken forever to cross the high seas. When we raced her around Sherkey the *Shira* won easily. O'Brien was a short man of great beam with a red beard, who went barefoot and wore nothing but a pair of shorts. His wife had not survived the rigours of ocean sailing. 'Poor thing,' we were told, 'she was very weak, was sick all the time. Could not stand it. Only lasted five years.'

Apart from the sailing, my father found time every year for some new project for the improvement of the island. Early on there was the year of the boathouse, followed by the year of the new pier, the year of the tennis court, made out of coral carried by Dinah, and the year of the swimming pool.

No Russian commissary could have been more meticulous about his plans for the swimming pool.

> The chosen site is at the top of the creek beside the vegetable garden, and near the tennis court. We have estimated that its depth should be about eleven feet and that it should be large enough for the springboard and possibly for another board. The men are digging at it and clearing the tons of mud and stones from it. I expect it to be completely cleared by Christmas and ready for the building of the wall with its sluice gates.

Phil and I were left to ourselves a good deal. When we were not sailing our dinghies or climbing the Dare Devil Rock we could play tennis or cricket, quarrelling much of the time. We raced on our bicycles over twisting coral paths and dared each other to cross the swaying suspension bridge at speed without falling in. Phil always won.

He was better at everything. 'It's easy,' he would explain when I tried to start the outboard engine. 'You're choking it with too much petrol.'

He would give it a pull and it would burst into life. At the diving board his elegant swallow dives contrasted with my painful belly flops.

'When you're running along the board, look out and not down at your feet.'

When Phil took to magic and gave a conjuror's performance for the adults one rainy day, my role was inferior. He dressed up as the Great Yossuf Ben Hassin for an exhibition of his magical powers. I was his unwilling slave Agar Agar, standing beside him in a dressing gown and turban, holding up objects for the great magician's attention as, in front of

129

applauding relatives and guest, my brother produced coloured handkerchiefs from a top hat.

'If you took the trouble to go through the magic book you might have been the Great Yossuf yourself.'

But I was only Agar Agar, standing to one side while the pound note disappeared, the shirt and tie went up in flames and the card tricks came out right. The finale was my execution preceded by sword passes through my body and the use of a bottle of red ink.

I can remember only one occasion when I got the better of Phil. After we were given a box of Turkish Delight it was I who wrote to Hadji Bey in Cork expressing my appreciation. By return I received another box, together with a letter and a photograph of the manufacturer wearing a tasselled fez and a beaded costume.

We went to Cork not long afterwards and found the small shop tucked beside the Metropole Hotel with its sign boasting A GOOD NAME IS WORTH MILLIONS. Hadji Bey was an Armenian who had fled Turkey and set up his business in Ireland in 1902. His shop was a paradise for anyone who had a sweet tooth and enjoyed that wobbly jelly doused in a snowstorm of white sugar.

Shyly I made myself known to him.

'You like my Turkish Delight? Honest to goodness, that makes me very happy.'

Around him were all those wooden boxes filled with sugared slices of Turkish Delight in pale red or white, some sprinkled with pistachio. And I was rewarded with yet another one. Disappointingly he was not wearing his costume, only ordinary clothes, and he spoke with a Cork accent.

He lasted there until 1972 when, to the sorrow of all Cork people and those who had the good fortune to have tasted his marvellous confectionery, his shop finally closed its doors. Perhaps Hadji Bey gave me my first interest in writing and in all things Eastern. Certainly the Great Yossuf and Agar Agar did not.

Straight across from the island was Reenafera, a large gabled house whose name meant 'Queen of the Sea', where many years later President de Gaulle was entertained. Before the Knowles bought the place Colonel Hartley lived there, making his garden and growing his gunnera. When he sold up to Colonel Knowles he had an auction. My father loved auctions, and he was able to buy two small cannon, a laundry basket, eighteen putting golf flags and a small rowing boat named *Colonel Arthur Hartley*. He also acquired a large anchor and chain, but before he could claim it, the anchor was carried away by Steve O'Casey, the all-in wrestler, the only man in the Kingdom of Kerry who could lift it.

The O'Casey brothers lived in an isolated farmhouse on a little peninsula separated by water from the Oysterbed Pier. All were enormous and stories of their strength and prowess and the buckets of potatoes they ate circulated around the neighbourhood. We had seen them in action at the annual Sneem regatta.

This took place every August. For weeks beforehand, we would watch four-oar and eight-oar rowing boats passing the island in training. On regatta day the Oysterbed became thick with men dressed in blue suits and caps. Out on the water the committee boat, an ancient trawler dressed with flags, bellowed contradictory orders from different members, primed with drink, shouting through microphones, as they fired guns and directed swimming races, the greasy pole with a pig as prize, and the rowing races. Along the lane running down to the pier stalls were put up by travellers, a fortune-teller, a shooting range, hot and cold drinks, women in black shawls with baskets of cakes and several fiddlers. There was also a man who invited anyone to a show of strength, a puny fellow compared to any of the O'Caseys.

The third year we were on the island all the O'Casey brothers were at the regatta, taking part in the main rowing race, Steve O'Casey among them. We watched them rowing out for the line in their frail craft. They were tackling a boat from Kilmakilloge, the harbour on the other side of the Kenmare River. The rivals were slow to arrive at the starting line and J.J.'s voice could be heard from the committee boat.

'I'd like to inform the world at large that the Kilmakilloge men have got cold feet!'

When the Kilmakilloge boat finally rowed up the crew were met with shouts of derision.

'They haven't a man among them!'

'Yerra, they're weaklings!'

'Give them hell!'

Certainly the men from the other side looked small compared to the giants with hard looks sitting in the Sneem boat who were feared throughout the Kingdom. With the signal to start the O'Casey brothers immediately took the lead. But the Kilmakilloge men were not giving up and were in hot pursuit as the boats neared Sherkey. They were out of our sight when the 'conflagration' took place – details of which were disputed ever after. Who rammed who and which of them picked up their oar and started the battle was never ascertained. In due course the O'Caseys came back with bruises and black eyes and crossed the line to cheers from the spectators, shouts from the committee boat and the boom of the gun. The Kilmakillogue men, also bruised and gashed, limped in five minutes later. A draw was never on the cards. And no boat had been capsised and no one had drowned.

My father knew he hadn't a chance of getting back his anchor. But he got interested in all-in wrestling and took us to Killarney for the world championship fought between Steve O'Casey and his deadly rival Danno O'Mahoney from Ballydehob in West Cork. Danno's father had emigrated many years ago to the United States and had returned; now, dressed like the prosperous American he was, he sat beside the ring, and all the way through the fight jumped up and down waving his arms, giving Danno and the referee constant advice.

It was a hideous fight and the crowd wanted O'Casey to win.

'Kill him!'

'Finish him, Steve!'

'Break him!'

'Give him the whip!'

'It's terrible cruel! I can't bear to look at it!' wailed the elderly woman beside my father, who could not take her eyes off the pair of them.

'Don't, then!' roared my father.

'It should not be allowed! I would be glad to pay to keep away from the next fight.'

'Pay me now,' he told her, 'and you needn't go.'

She shook her head and went on looking throughout the eighteen rounds of five minutes with one minute intervals.

The fight was rougher and a lot less choreographed than

those wrestling bouts that appeared on television many decades later. There were not many rules – the two champions thumped and banged each others heads on the floor and from time to time threw each other out of the ring. Once two O'Casey brothers grabbed O'Mahoney and prevented him climbing back. The battle raged back and forth, but in every clinch Danno came out superior. On four or five occasions he held Steve in a grip from which the gong alone saved the Kerry man. Sometimes he would hold Steve in an impossible knot, spit complacently on the floor and give a happy nod to his father. In one grip he held an O'Casey arm so that there was complete obstruction of the blood supply to the hand for some time.

At the eighteenth round Danno started throwing Steve about seriously. Six times he picked him up and threw him to the ground, remaining standing himself. Then they got into a clinch and by some peculiar manoeuvre Danno fell out of the ring. He gripped the rope when falling and, turning over, his back hit the side of the ring which was projecting and then he fell a good ten feet to the ground, which was hard and covered with sharp gravel.

This blow and fall finished him and, although he got back into the ring on time, Steve hit and battered him about so that he could never recover. We all agreed (when we were out of earshot) that Danno was by far the best wrestler, who only lost through bad luck. Too bad – it was Steve O'Casey who was the world champion all-in wrestler.

The match gave Phil an idea. We would stage our own contest. I did not think this was a good plan at all. Only recently I had tussled with him and fell off the balcony cutting open my head. My father was away on a cruise and

Dr O'Sullivan was fetched.

Dr O'Sullivan was a last resort, a small dark man with a shifty manner, well known for his habit of throwing himself out of rhododendron bushes at passing cars.

When he was rowed over from the Oysterbed he was sober, but very dirty. 'And what's the little fellow done now?' he asked as if I had deliberately harmed myself. Blood was sticky on my face. We watched him open his bag and my mother suggested he might like to wash his hands.

'Oh, that won't be necessary.' He sewed me up and I have the scar. Now Phil wanted another fight.

My mother suggested a sailing race instead.

'Boring!' said Phil and I felt I had to echo 'Boring!'

'What about a prize to catch the largest amount of fish?'

'We don't need any more fish.'

Unfortunately my father approved.

'It's time they grew up, Joyce.'

'Not wrestling!' There was silence as we remembered the look of Danno after Steve O'Casey had finished with him.

'No – how about a fight with quarterstaffs?'

'What?'

The bamboo my mother had planted three years ago had grown large. He cut two canes and trimmed them down to size.

A rough ring was set outside the house and my parents and their friends gathered to watch. We stripped to the waist.

'All right, boys. When I blow the whistle you can begin.'

Almost before the whistle sounded Phil gave me a crack over the neck which set me gasping. I responded with one over his shins.

A few more blows resulted in a sprained ankle, a bleeding nose and an intervention from Bruin who rushed into the ring and seized my pole.

'Enough!' The audience was not enjoying the spectacle. The great Danno and Steve had lasted eighteen rounds but we only went three.

'It's not fair!' Phil complained. Although I had no broken ribs, victory had been slipping to him, but he was not allowed the conqueror's role. The spectators clapped nervously as my father in his role as referee took possession of our staves. His diary entry read: 'Quarterstaff match between Phil and Peter. Match drawn as both were nearly killed.'

9

The Garden Cottage

I N THE LATE THIRTIES our Irish boyhood was suspended for a time.

As a surgeon my father did a good deal of work operating on patients who suffered the awful consequences of TB. Much research had been done abroad, particularly in Sweden which he visited, becoming immensely impressed by the medical facilities that he saw there. As a result he considered that Sweden was a forward looking country and Phil and I would benefit by living in a practical and well organised society. He decided that instead of going to an English public school like Hailybury, which he had loathed, we should get a proper European education and become fluent in European languages.

Like everything he did that concerned us he did not consult us.

Our first reaction was joy. 'That means we don't have to go back to Baymount – Castle Park.'

In the early summer of 1939 we travelled to Sweden in order to attend Sigtuna, one of the country's few private boarding schools. Before the term began we went to different families to learn some basic Swedish.

'During that time I don't want you to meet each other. Is that clear? This isn't a holiday.'

My host and hostess were a Major in the Swedish army and his wife. They had two tow-headed sons, Carl and Nolle. The Major was a small, bald, stockily built, middle-aged man with a white moustache which he was forever twisting with his fingers. He had some sort of post at the Royal Palace and each morning would depart dressed in his uniform.

Two days after I arrived he took us along to the Palace to see King Gustav.

'An honour, something you will never forget.'

The old king was in white flannels playing tennis. His opponent was a lot younger, but the king managed to beat him and there was a ripple of applause from the watching spectators.

'He always wins,' Carl said, clapping hard. Sweden might be a democratic society, but King Gustav's courtiers knew how to behave.

I have another memory of drunken middle-aged men dressed in plus-fours staggering around a square in Gothenburg under the midnight sun. But before our Swedish education could begin war threatened and we were sent home. So I never got to Sigtuna, never mastered three or four languages, or acquired a liking for smoked and raw fish. Only two Swedish words have stayed with me, *maast*, meaning yogurt, and the word everyone knows, *smorgasbord*. I see that it has a place in the Oxford Dictionary: 'n. Swedish hors-d'oeuvre meal with variety of dishes. (Sw. *smor* butter, *gas* goose, lump of butter, *bord* table.)'

It was back to our dismal prep schools.

While we were away my grandfather died in his ninety-fifth year. We would no longer live in Farmhill which was let to the British government as a residence for their diplomatic representatives in Ireland, beginning with Sir John Maffey, later Lord Rugby who tussled with de Valera throughout the War. These diplomats, together with their wives and staff, hated Farmhill's cold rooms, and throughout their lease, which lasted for twenty years, complained incessantly. Uncle Paddy began calling his dogs after them; there was a succession of whining restless liver and white spaniels – Maffey, Laithwaite, Clutterbuck and Tory.

From now on our home would be Laragh.

By 1938 Laragh House Hotel offered guests thirty-six bedrooms, two bars, including the special cocktail bar, a billiard room, and the ballroom. At first every thing went well, and people responded to the advertisements that were placed in the *Irish Tatler* and the *Irish Times*.

LARAGH HOUSE LTD ANNAMOE, CO WICKLOW.
The Most Beautiful Sports Hotel in Ireland.
Golf, Shooting, Riding, Hard Court Tennis.
H and C in all Rooms. Open all year round. Fully licensed.
DANCE every Saturday (Band) in New Ballroom.
The Perfect Place for the Perfect Party.
Telephone Glendalough 4 or write for Particulars.

The *Irish Tatler* informed its readers that Laragh 'is far enough from the City to attract the fastidious who seek a restful few hours. But I hear that the comfort of the hotel is its chief attraction.'

The *Irish Tatler* added that

The Directors have been fortunate enough in securing the services of Mr Guy Melville Barker ... educated at Westminster

School, London, and Trinity College Cambridge . . . took his Bar finals . . . then forsook the Bar for an Hotel career . . . Rouen – Hotel de la Poste – Grosvenor House . . . Hyde Park Hotel – started the Coconut Grove and ran Brummels in Albemarle Street.

My mother had no suspicions as to why he should leave such prestigious places for an obscure post in County Wicklow. Alas, he did not stay for long, but departed one Monday with the weekend's takings. My mother missed 'dear Mr Barker'.

She had no better luck with Monsieur Goudal who applied for the post of head chef. When she interviewed the tall languorous Frenchman dressed in a pinstriped suit, he made a good impression. His moustache twitched as he spoke French. Her command of the language was uncertain, but when in doubt she said '*peut-être*' which could mean yes or no.

'Such a charming man!'

Monsieur Goudal had been head chef of the South African Railways, then sauce cook at the Carlton, and his last post had been at the House of Commons. Sadly, when he came to Laragh he proved to have a ferocious temper. After he attacked one of the scullery maids with a carving knife, my mother could never quite accept that he was in the wrong.

'She must have annoyed him. French people can get very emotional, particularly over food.'

On 3 September 1939 we were on the island where we gathered round the wireless and listened to Chamberlain's gravelly voice on the radio announcing that England was at war. Immediately my father and my Uncle Becher decided to join the British army medical services. Uncle Paddy was the one brother who would stay in Ireland.

In the late autumn of 1939 my father supervised the pulling up and dismantling of his fleet for the duration of the war. The punts and most of the rowboats were put away, and the newly acquired *Kingfisher* was floated onto a cradle, hauled up on a winch and hoisted above high tide. More difficult was the *Shira*, which took up too much room to be berthed near the island. After a long search a place was found for her down the Kenmare River. Mr Cotter, the postman at Blackwater Bridge, agreed to look after her. He had always admired her and had written a lengthy poem in her honour which he used to recite in his beautiful accent,

> The pride of Kerry, the queen of Kenmare,
> Ye sailors know it is true,
> The *Shira* is the finest craft
> To cross the ocean blue;
> From lovely Sneem to fair Kinsale
> She gaily spreads her snow white sail.

Now she was stripped of gear, together with blankets, cooking pots, and books which Dinah carried up to the house in her cart. The mast had to be taken out; Mr Skinner was brought all the way from his shipyard in Baltimore with his people and gave 'a beautiful example of skill, safety and complete control in which every man knew his job and did it'. Then the *Shira* was floated down the Kenmare River to Blackwater Bridge where she remained for five years. Brosnan was sacked − or, to put it more kindly, 'let go'.

In the spring of 1940 we went to the island for a last visit before my father departed. He took down a large group of friends and deployed his guests with his usual energy – digging drains, playing tennis and catching mackerel with feathers from the *Memphis*, which, apart from our dinghies, was the last of our boats that remained on the water.

On the day before he left there was a fall of heavy snow on the mountains and in the clear sunny morning the white Kerry mountains contrasting with the deep blue sea around us were most beautiful. It was an image that he would take away with him and retain in Africa and the Middle East.

From now on my mother would manage the farm with the aid of a farm manager and steward, and keep the hotel open for a few summer months. Very soon petrol became unavailable, and this had a drastic effect on the numbers of guests coming to Laragh. But even in the most austere period of the Emergency a trickle of visitors managed to make their way out into remote Wicklow. They included a number of English visitors who made their way across the Irish Sea, avoiding German U-boats, in order to eat meat. There was none in England, so we were told. The hotel offered them mutton and beef which was also available to daring Catholics, tired of eating fish on Fridays. As one of the kitchen hands put it, 'One man eats a big mouthful of meat, and the other the tail end of a fish.'

Guests could also enjoy the dancing. We would watch them through the large plate glass windows of the new ballroom when a special band from Dublin came down. Des Fitzgerald, and Jimmy Byrne the footballer, who played the drums, wore red tuxedos, had their hair plastered with Brylcreem and played waltzes, foxtrots and the occasional rumbas and tangos.

We picked out the pretty girls.

'Look at that one – she's OK. But look who she's dancing with!' To our eyes the men were invariably old and wrinkled. How could any young girl with any sense bear to be with them? The spectacle of ancient Lotharios in the arms of bubbly young beauties never lost its interest. Sometimes a girl would see us with our noses pressed against the glass and smile.

After we outgrew our prep schools we were sent to St Columba's in the Dublin mountains, which, because of the war, attracted numerous boys who in ordinary circumstances would have gone off to public schools in England. Many of the masters were unusual people, gifted if not eccentric and through the influence of men like Peter Alt, Brian Boydell and Mark Mortimer, we tended to be more interested in art than games. The school figures in the novels of its most prominent ex-pupils, my contemporaries, William Trevor and Michael Campbell.

In the holidays we would go from Rathfarnham into Dublin and take the train to Rathdrum, where my mother would meet us in the dog cart. Trunks and bags were tucked away in the back, and the pony would trot to Laragh, through the Vale of Clara with its thick woods and river, then to Laragh village, a bridge and a dozen houses, and the long climb home.

Away from school those first few hours were golden.

'What shall we do tomorrow?'

For convenience the three of us lived in one of the half dozen cottages scattered around the estate, together with Molly, the cook general and retailer of gossip. The Garden Cottage was overcrowded and damp and, as with every place where my mother lived, the little drawing room smelt of dog. There were four dogs at this time, and Prickles the white

Persian cat, who was almost as hairy as Bruin. When it rained, we were crowded in there with dust, animal hairs, my mother's tapestry, bills and farm accounts, books and magazines. Throughout the war we subscribed to the *Illustrated London News*, the *Spectator*, the *Listener* and *Country Life* which stayed in its time warp and persistently published studies of snowy hillsides and Cotswolds villages for the salvation of which my father and uncle had joined the British army. Such magazines kept my mother in touch with the outside world.

In the evening we would play cards or listen to the radio, always the English news, the ritual of Big Ben followed by various Allied national anthems and the measured tones of the newsreader. We did not go as far as standing up for 'God Save the King' as did some of the families of my friends. 'Turn it off,' my mother would say if losses of Allied ships and bombing raids were too bleak. Occasionally to our delight, we picked up Lord Haw Haw, but we never got to hear our neighbour, Francis Stuart, who was also broadcasting for the Germans.

The bedroom Phil and I shared had weeping walls which were like waterfalls in winter; in the morning our sheets were spotted with dew.

'A little bit of damp won't do you any harm,' my mother said, unworried by the fact that there was scarcely a local family round us that was not threatened by TB.

Meanwhile Molly would treat us with home remedies – Friar's Balsam for colds, gooseberry thorns for blisters and hot poultices for anything else. The old drunk doctor only called with his bag of medicines in cases of emergency. How many drunken GPs practised in the Ireland of that time? On one occasion when I had a high temperature and some unusual symptoms, Dr Cotter dismissed my mother and Molly who were hovering at the door. A thin man with a long cadaverous face, when the door was closed he sat on the edge of my bed staring at me intently.

'Have you been with any women?'

I was twelve years old. I shook my head.

'I want you to think very carefully.'

He took my temperature and before he left warned me that I should have no more contact with the opposite sex.

'Oh, for God's sake,' said Phil later, after he had a look. 'You've got mumps in the balls.' And so it proved to be. For a time Molly pampered me with hot broth and special apple pie with flaky pastry. When the doctor returned he agreed, yes, perhaps it was mumps after all.

Molly was small and dark-haired, with a habit of suddenly falling on her knees to say a quick prayer. The walls of her little room were covered with pictures of saints and the Sacred Heart and rather than dust the sitting room she would spray on a bit of holy water from her own personal stoup. Before she came to us she had worked as a lady's maid to a woman who was a kleptomaniac; every time they went out shopping it was Molly's duty to return all the stolen goods to the manager.

Now she would stand at the door of the kitchen with her arms folded and tell tales to my mother. 'Madam, O'Reilly spent the afternoon asleep in the orchard.' 'Madam, there's butter gone missing from the dairy.'

'Oh, yes, Molly?' Like my grandfather listening to Miss Moore's stories, my mother never took notice.

Molly and my mother shared a love of animals. The pet lamb, so pretty and frisky, that Molly fed in the spring, blew

145

up into a monster the size of a sheep from overeating, head-butting us whenever we tried to enter the kitchen. For a time he would follow us around the house, bumping into furniture, and once he broke a *famille rose* plate. My mother found him a new home with our Aunt Sammy out at her beautiful Georgian house.

'How's Mr Lamb?' we asked at the beginning of the summer holidays. Both my mother and Molly spluttered with rage.

'Isn't he after being eaten?' For all her protests about food and waste and wartime, the aunt was never forgiven.

Love of animals meant primarily love of horses and the war-time shortage of petrol went some way towards alleviating my mother's loneliness. She did not mind the absence of cars at all. Horse-power was important once again, and the stables in the two large yards were full of farm horses and under-exercised riding horses.

Every morning at eight the farm bell would ring and groups of men would appear and vanish into the surrounding woods and fields. I can still see their faces and hear their slow Wicklow voices. Indoors and out we employed around forty people on minuscule wages. There were ploughmen and dairymen, a dairymaid who made yellow butter, a hen boy, and various gardeners. There was the hotel staff. There were farm workers like Paddy Nolan who lived with his family in the neat cut-stone lodge at the main entrance to Laragh. Arthur O'Neill, the hall porter, was at the back gate lodge. The lodges were similar to those at Farmhill.

From the village other men would come up every day, Paddy Moran, who dug in the garden, and Dan Byrne, who worked in the dairy and every two months was called in and paid with twenty cigarettes to cut our hair with scissors and shears as part of my father's drive for self-sufficiency. He might be in Africa, but his ideas were still carried out. We had our own flickering and unreliable electricity, our own butter and meat, and in summer men were sent up to our bog to cut and stack the turf. They went fearfully, because the bog had an elemental, known as the Great Boo, whose groans and smell added zest to the working day.

Every week, Bill O'Reilly, the steward, came into the drawing room to discuss the farming calendar. Tall and taciturn, he lived in yet another of the estate cottages. On other occasions he would stand in the hall of the Garden Cottage discussing with my mother the latest problems, while Molly listened behind the kitchen door. A broken machine, a man who had gone off on a bender, which cattle to send to the fair, O'Reilly would deal with them all. The minute he had left Molly would emerge from the kitchen.

'Madam, I heard what O'Reilly mentioned about the pigs.'

'Oh?'

'There were six piglets when I last passed the pen. Now there are only four ...'

'Oh?'

'That new man was seen in the lower yard watching the sows. He had no right to be there.'

'Ah.'

The brooding mountains and hills capped with silky grey clouds were forever dripping down on us. In winter the rain fell hour after hour, the fields were waterlogged, the streams overflowed and the mist settled.

When it cleared, we would still be saying, 'What shall we do now?'

My mother would say, 'Take out Jacky and Pav?'

Jacky the half-hunter had a habit of suddenly turning his head and giving you a savage bite when you were in were in the process of putting on his saddle. But riding Pav was a far worse ordeal. The daily race to the stables between Phil and myself became increasingly desperate, because the last one to reach the yard had to ride the ex-polo pony. Saddling up, tightening the girths, inserting the bit into a champing unwilling mouth, getting into the saddle as the horse moved away, were preliminaries to an hour of terror.

Pav – short for Pavlova – was grey with soulful black eyes and the action of a skier, going this way and that as she pretended to be following a ball. She had an ability that never failed of catching you by surprise by shying at a stone, a fir cone, a blackbird, anything that set her eyes rolling.

In the riding field my mother had put in a series of jumps, a gorse bank, poles and a water jump. Surrounded by her dogs she would come down and watch us. Occasionally a dog would rush out and harry a horse just as it was about to jump. In Pav's case, this was not often, as she would refuse with a violent swerve.

'Face her directly at the jump and be firm!'

Another swerve, another refusal, and quite often I would fall.

'She is only remembering her polo days . . .'

Nor did we like the way Pav bucked when she had enough, or her habit of bolting for her stable on the way home, head down, tail wildly frisking, while the person on her back hung on like John Gilpin. In the yard she made up her mind either to throw the rider off at the water trough or go full speed for her stable; unless you ducked you were liable to break your neck, like Mr Booth hanged from the chandelier.

After exercising the horses, we would still be complaining about having nothing to do. We were spoiled darlings, living on an eight-hundred acre estate with four tennis courts, two golf courses, a lake to swim in and horses to ride. Beyond the immediate environment of the hotel were two woods which in spring were filled with bluebells and primroses.

My mother would say, 'Go and climb Trooperstown', and we would set off with the dogs. Trooperstown was just opposite and it was not very high. But each little rise was followed by another. We would wade through tussocky gorse and the mountainy landscape beloved by John Synge, and return in an exhausted condition to Molly's hard scones and cakes, wet dogs and quickly fading light.

Or we would play golf. We got the odd lesson from Kelly, one of the professionals, who, even in the midst of the Emergency, was employed to teach the ever-scarcer guest.

'You're cheating.'

'I'm not.'

'I saw you – I saw you!'

It was not that easy to pick up a ball from the the long grass and throw it on the green without being spotted. Balls were scarce and had to be treasured. We had one or two at the most and found it hard, even with Kelly at our side, to keep one or the other within the swathes of horse-mown grass. Hours would be spent searching for balls played into the rough, which consisted of gorse, bracken, heather and rabbit holes into which they trickled.

'All right, you win.'

'We've only played two holes.'

'I'm not going on.'

'Spoil sport!'

Swimming in our own private lake should have been anyone's dream. Here again, my father had shown his energy and enthusiasm. The dark stretch of water ringed by pine trees and rhododendrons had been transformed with balconies, specially created paddling pools for children, diving boards, changing rooms, and on one of the islands in the lake a high platform had been positioned where the foolhardy could jack-knife or somersault into the freezing coal black water. Every year the surrounding trees dropped their leaves and other slimy things on the muddy bottom. Wearing our new Jantzen bathing costumes we would emerge shivering from the changing rooms.

'You go first.'

'Coward!' And we would wrestle to throw one another into the frigid lake whose colour never varied from deepest mourning black. On the hottest day with a clear blue sky above, the water was always unbearably cold. By comparison the sea off the Kenmare River were positively steaming.

We took little part in the running of the farm.

'Darling, I wonder if you could collect the eggs?'

I enjoyed my own gaudy brood of bantams, the little bright coloured cocks with their eunuchs' crow, and the ridiculous Polish bantams, their eyes covered like miniature Bruins. But my mother's hens hated me and only by lifting up their rears with the end of a spade could I retrieve an egg without being savagely pecked.

Cows were milked and fields were ploughed by the many men we employed and in the social climate of the day we were not expected to dirty our hands. Only at harvest time did we help to stook the oats or the wheat which the farm was forced to grow on thin Wicklow land because of Emergency regulations. Then we would watch the steam thresher slowly make its way up the avenue and into the long field, where for two or three days the men would work enveloped in clouds of steam. Each man had his duty, varying from watching the whirling belts to pitchforking up the corn. But we were spectators.

Jimmy Connolly was the rabbiter who set off every morning with his bag of ferrets and his greyhound. He worked full time at the slaughter. He was a small dark-haired man who never changed his clothes; once, we were told, he had been a champion runner for Wicklow.

We would follow him out to a vast rabbit town. The whole estate was covered with their burrows, including the golf courses, where the bunnies joyfully dug in the mown grass and the sandy bunkers. We would watch them sunning themselves at the edge of a hole or scampering across the grass. Many places called to mind Cousin Edith's description: 'I thought the face of the field was running away from me.'

In Mantegna's *Agony in the Garden* the artist has painted six rabbits, along with the sleeping apostles and kneeling Christ. Whenever I go to London's National Gallery and look at that picture and read the title I remember the rabbits at Laragh playing havoc among the vegetables.

Connolly would put his ear to the ground.

'There's a dozen little bastards down there.' He was seldom wrong. The red-eyed ferrets would slide into the holes like snakes for the thumping squeak and shriek and killing.

'She's right, isn't she?' He would point at the scores of corpses laid out in rows like old-fashioned pictures of shooting parties. By the time he had made his rounds of seven or eight burrows, the first would have bred a new generation waiting for his ferrets.

Far too many would be sent to the Garden Cottage for Molly to cook.

'Rabbit yesterday, rabbit today and rabbit tomorrow,' we chanted at mealtimes. They had been served up quite often at Farmhill, but to nothing like the same extent as they were in our cottage in Laragh.

The rest of Laragh's rabbits were sent to Wales.

'The poor bloody Welsh are mad for them.' Their meat was rationed and their catchers had gone off to war. By 1944 the price of rabbits had risen to four and six pence each, which Connolly pocketed. Since his wages were around two pounds, he got the same amount for nine rabbits. They must have been gamey by the time they arrived at Holyhead.

Occasionally we would make a foray into Dublin. In spite of wartime restrictions, the blue St Kevin's bus, packed with country women dressed in black, holding enormous bags, and men in dark blue suits and caps, regularly made the journey from Glendalough to Dublin. We were bucketed around like a ship in a storm as we sped through bog land fringed with mountains wrapped in mist. There was always the moment on Calary bog when when the bus crossed a small bridge without slowing down, and the people who were standing hit their heads against the metal roof.

The best journeys to Dublin were those when my mother took the dog cart. For the thirty-mile drive we wrapped up warmly as we climbed in beside her. Within the high varnished sides, above the big wheels, she would sit up holding the reins over the brass rail, directing Jacky or Pav as they trotted between the shafts, curry-combed, satin skin gleaming.

Slowly we would cross Calary to the place where on Stephen's Day we attended the point-to-point in the wind and the rain. My mother would not have missed the point-to-point for the world. Moving among weather-beaten faces, gumboots and blackthorn sticks, we would follow her around the various jumps and banks, the dark clouds scudding the hills.

'Put your money on Jim Byrne's horse,' she would say, giving us each a half-crown. And Jim Byrne's horse usually won.

But on the summer days when we drove to Dublin there were no crowds, only the long silence beyond Laragh's walls. There was no traffic, nothing in the world apart from a stray cyclist battling the wind or a farmer with his flock of black-faced sheep blocking the twisting road ahead of us. Before the dog cart dipped down beside the Big Sugarloaf we would stop and open the picnic basket for hard boiled eggs, and perhaps some tinned salmon, while no picnic was complete without some triangles of Mitchelstown cheese. Meanwhile my mother would light the Volcano kettle for tea, stuffing twigs and pieces of paper into the little chimney in the outside jacket that boiled the water. Recently I was delighted to read that the Volcano has been revived as an essential for camping.

We moved on and at the bottom of the big hill at Kilmacanogue we were on the flat and civilisation was in sight; Laragh, the dark lonely lake of Glendalough and the mountains were well behind us. The last fifteen miles over empty roads went smoothly and swiftly until we reached the centre of Dublin. Outside the Shelbourne the coach-and-four provided by the hotel would be waiting to take guests out to Lucan. (*Dublin Opinion* had an old man saying: 'It's just what

I said way back in 1903, these motor cars are only a passing phase.')

We trotted into Merrion Square and Goffs where the dog cart and pony were stabled. For the rest of the day there was shopping at Brown Thomas and Switzers and the rare opportunity of going to the cinema, a night at the deserted house in Fitzwilliam Place and, next morning, the dog cart filled up with bags of shopping, we made the long journey home. My mother was always glad to be going back, while we always felt dejected.

We had few friends up in the hills. We did not meet the Childers boys whose father, Robert Childers, had in 1941 arranged a secret meeting at neighbouring Glendalough House which resulted in liaison arrangements between Great Britain and Ireland in the case of a German invasion of southern Ireland. Down the road behind the high stone walls of Laragh Castle was a boy of our age, Michael Stuart, but we were not allowed to play with him; Michael's mother was that free spirit, Isolde, daughter of Maud Gonne MacBride, while his father was living in Germany, working for the Reich.

One evening Molly leant against the kitchen door and announced, 'Madam a man in a black beret with a foreign accent has called at the back door of the hotel and asked Major Mandeville the way to the Stuarts.'

Major Mandeville, the retired British army veteran who managed the hotel at the time, immediately informed the guards. The foreigner turned out to be a German secret agent, Captain Hermann Goertz, who had parachuted into Meath with twenty thousand American dollars in his pocket and his First World War medals. He walked southwards into Wicklow, swimming the Boyne on the way. By the time he got to our hotel and went on to Laragh Castle he was starving. Mrs Stuart tried to help him but he was caught and interned. Forty years later I was told that Goertz camped for a while in a hut on our back avenue; my informant had looked into the hut where there were clothes hanging up to dry. Perhaps that is true; the avenue, two miles from the hotel, was not frequented much in those days. Phil and I seldom went near it.

We would not have minded more contact with Michael Stuart. Everyone else in our restricted circle was old or odd.

Mrs Taylor lived in a derelict house surrounded by peacocks and goats. 'Don't please pull the chain,' she would call out if you wished to go to the lavatory. 'The pipes are still not connected.' Ralph Cusack, a well-known Dublin painter, bought a house called 'Uplands', which was reputed to have the steepest avenue in Ireland. Ralph marketed rare bulbs and plants in catalogues that became famous for their lush prose, while his exploits when he was drunk were legendary. Eventually he retired to France where he wrote a good picaresque novel, *Cadenza*; I treasure my copy.

A bon viveur like Ralph was not likely to run up against two schoolboys. What was far more likely was that we would be invited to take tea with Mrs Penrose, who lived opposite us in one of the houses where John Synge's family spent their holidays. Behind the long Georgian front the red window blinds were never pulled back, so that the interior was always a subdued crimson dusk.

Mrs Penrose had the hallmarks of the Anglo-Irish eccentric, dogs – little furry ones, untrustworthy Pekingese with bulging eyes and yappy terriers – cats – once when I went upstairs to the bathroom I found the basin full of new born kittens – and buckets under the leaks in the roof. She spoke an Edwardian schoolgirl's dialect in a high-pitched voice.

'I say, isn't it too jolly, Monty beating Rommel like that!'

She liked the odd French proverb; 'I say, Joyce, "*C'est le premier pas qui coute*".'

'*Peut-être.*'

Followed by her dogs – ours were all left behind shut up howling in stables – we would be led through the hall, where on the table was a parcel stamped and addressed, which over the years was never sent. The drawing room was immense and cold, as only one of the two fireplaces was ever lit. It was also as crammed with furniture as an auction room, giving it the atmosphere much sought after by recent interior decorators of shabby chic. Among the chairs and tables was a treadle sewing machine. Here, watched by her ancestors and over-looked by a Venetian painting which today would probably be worth a million, we would take tea, off a tarnished silver tray brought in by a maid wearing a piece of newspaper folded into a cocked paper hat.

An hour of boredom would have to be spent eating cakes and sandwiches made out of murky Emergency bread and flour, listening to my mother and her hostess discuss problems of country living – colic in horses, maids, compulsory tillage, people dying.

'Poor Mrs Byrne. I hear she's very seedy.'

Occasionally a head would turn in our direction.

'How do you like your new school? I'm sure its spiffing.'

Mrs Penrose's red-faced daughter, Diana, would appear in her jodhpurs and gumboots.

'Oh, for God's sake, mother, not all the old silver. Joyce and the boys don't want that sort of thing.'

Diana would sit down with her legs out at an angle and

silently wolf sandwiches one after the other, before lighting a cigarette and stomping off to feed potatoes and slimy garbage to her pigs. A year or two later she fled to England and joined the Women's Land Army and – amazingly – got married.

Mrs Penrose's son came home, invalided out of the British army. Going to tea became more exciting because sometimes we would be greeted by Stephen standing between the pillars of the front door aiming a shotgun at us.

'Poor darling, it's his nervous breakdown after fighting in Africa. Silly Billy!'

We also took tea with Archdeacon Synge, the brother of the playwright. We enjoyed going to the rectory at Annamoe – later the home of the film director, John Boorman – because the Archdeacon would take us upstairs to see his bats hanging from the rafters of the roof. He was proud of them, and talked to them as if they were his children – much more gently than to his daughter Edith who acted as his housekeeper.

Archdeacon Samuel Synge had gone to China just before the Boxer Rebellion as the first Church of Ireland minister ordained for the Church Missionary Society. For years he journeyed across the province of Fu-Kien in his role as itinerant missionary doctor before returning to Ireland in 1914 and becoming rector of Annamoe and Derrylossery. Although he had shed some of the fierce piety associated with the Plymouth Brethren which had made his famous brother's life a misery, he had firm views on a number of topics, like Hell and Salvation. Two things obsessed him, the iniquity of lipstick and the evils of Guinness. My mother always wore lipstick, and her brother was a director of Guinness' Brewery. The Archdeacon would be polite enough to us at home in his rectory, but she was vulnerable when we went to church.

The Garden Cottage

The church at Derrylossery, a pretty eighteenth-century shoe box with wheezing organ, mouldy walls and horse-box pews, catered for half a dozen Protestant families. Later, during the fifties the roof was taken off by vandals representing the Church of Ireland. When President Childers died he was brought up the long hill at Kilmacanogue and over Calary to lie beside its shell.

Winter and summer my mother would drive us there in the governess cart. 'Don't suck any sweets,' she would say as she closed the door of our box.

Inside we sat in our private world, invisible to the rest of the small congregation, each family enjoying the same isolation. We sang hymns and heard prayers, but could see nothing of what was going on until the Archdeacon suddenly appeared in the pulpit above us, his huge white beard spread like a prophet's.

Phil and I would already have made our bet.

'He did Guinness last week.'

'Ssh . . .'

We listened intently as he began to address his tiny flock. 'I want to speak to you today about an unfortunate habit which I have noticed even here in this beautiful corner of Wicklow.' He paused. 'I mention lipstick . . .' The word, proclaimed loudly, trembled on his lips and around the bare walls of the church.

Phil kicked me on the shins. He had won again.

10

Buried Treasure

LIFE WAS SUBDUED when my father wasn't there. It was strange going to the island without him and his friends and his plans.

The first time we went petrol was still available. Molly came as well to cook for us.

'Has Madam remembered to bring a supply of candles?'

At the last moment we squeezed the usual crate of hens, plus my bantams, into the back. They had been rounded up the night before with the aid of the hen boy who, surrounded by barking dogs, climbed to the top of trees where they were roosting.

The dogs panted as they looked out of the windows, Prickles scratched in her basket, while the hens were quiet for most of the time. We made the familiar journey, driving through Limerick and stopping for a picnic and the ceremonial lighting of the Volcano.

'There are the Reeks!'

The highlight of any journey to the island was the moment south of Limerick when the jagged line of mountains sheltering Killarney first shot up in the air. After Castleisland they filled the whole horizon. We motored into Killarney and stopped for the night at the Lake Hotel where the management and staff had become used to our visits, and everything was done to accommodate our party and our livestock. Because of the times there were few guests.

Next morning we descended to the great hall surrounded by antlered heads and into the dining room where we had the usual magnificent breakfast, apart from the Camp Coffee which already was the wartime substitute for the real thing. Afterwards the porter came in with a doleful face and spoke to my mother.

'She's escaped?'

Upstairs three maids in tight black pinafore dresses and lace caps were gazing out of the window to where Prickles was staring back from a ridge top overlooking mountains and lake.

Theoretically at least Prickles was mine.

'I'll get her.'

I crawled out to grab her but she distanced herself a few more feet away and, even sitting astride the ridge tiles, when I looked down I found the drop down to the ground terrifying. It was a relief when my mother ordered me back in.

'Let her make up her own mind. I don't want to have to take you to hospital if you fall.' The graveyard was more likely than the hospital.

'Please, Madam, excuse me . . .' One of the maids pulled up her black dress and, before we could stop her, skipped out of the window and in half a minute was halfway out on the roof. We watched her climb the steep incline of slates, grab the cat and bring her back to her basket.

'That was most kind,' said my mother.

'Sure, Ma'am, it was nothing. Last year an old gentleman sat out there in his pyjamas.'

'Good heavens!'

'He was babbling about the beauties of Killarney. It took the fire brigade to get him down.'

Later we drove over the mountains to Sneem and the Oysterbed where Jerry was waiting for us with the *Memphis*. The tide was out and thick oozy mud with tendrils of seaweed clung to the sides of the boat with a magnetic force. While crabs scuttled for safety across the mud, there was nothing we could do. The little *Memphis*, laden like Noah's Ark, had to wait for two hours for the water to lift her.

Jerry seized two oars and Phil and I one each, and we rowed across to the island where the absence of my father was palpable. Even with Jerry and Denis to tend us and Molly to cook for us, everything was much more difficult without him telling us all what to do. But my mother had her plans. We hardly had time to explore old haunts when she called us into the sitting room.

'If the Germans come we will hole up here.' Was this why she had brought down the bantams which were pets in the same way as the dogs, while the hens were walking eggs and meat?

'We'll spend the next few days getting supplies. Not a word to Jerry or Denis.'

'Why not?'

'The fewer people who know the better.'

'Will we stay here the whole time?'

'I think so. If the news gets bad.'

'What about Molly?' As usual, after cooking for us and washing up, Molly had retired to the little house on her own so she couldn't hear us talking.

'Oh, we'll see about Molly.'

We agreed that this plan was wonderful. Perhaps my

mother was intimidated at the thought of running Laragh for the foreseeable future and considered that living on the island was a means of escaping the dour responsibility of the estate and the hotel. Perhaps she felt that in this way she could demonstrate solidarity with my father and the Allied effort. Or she may have been a romantic at heart.

The next week was spent rowing over to the Oysterbed, and taking the car to Sneem and Kenmare in order to buy supplies. I have memories of the cartons of tins which Phil and I rowed over during those long summer evenings when the men had gone home. (Don't tell Jerry! Don't tell Denis!) In the twilight Carnation Milk, peaches, sardines, pilchards, corned beef and salmon were lugged up from the pier, across the slippery seaweed, through the avenue of rhododendrons and up to the house. More importantly, we acquired cans of paraffin oil.

Soon all the little cabins of the house were full of tinned food and paraffin. Much good trying to keep the secret from Molly. However it gave her a sense of power not to tell the secret to Jerry and Denis.

My mother said, 'I want you and Peter to bury everything around the island at night.'

'Everything?'

'There's enough here to keep us for months. We'll make a map.'

I can see her in the sitting room, paper spread in front of her, making a rough outline of the island and marking the location of our hoard with crosses. We watched and offered advice as to where things should go. The precious cans of paraffin were to be buried in the garden near the house, the tins of sardines near the Dare Devil Cave and the Carnation

Milk would go behind the tennis court. She put in cross-references and clues. 'Five yards from nearest palm tree to the south side of turf shed.'

For the rest of the summer we went out every evening after Jerry and Denis had rowed off to the mainland. Apart from Molly peering out of the kitchen window into the dusk, the cat and dogs were the only invited spectators as we worked until darkness fell and then continued with the aid of a torch and a storm lantern. On two nights the digging had to be done in rain; the thick mud sucked in the crates and it was like burying coffins. If a guard had seen us he would have associated our activities with the manufacture of poteen.

'Do be careful, dear – we don't want anyone else to discover footprints and that sort of thing.'

I don't remember how we planned to feed the dogs. In those days tins of dog food were scarce, if available at all. There was always mackerel, caught from lines trailed from our dinghies.

'When do we open them?' we asked, as another twenty tins of peaches sank into the dark soil.

'When the Germans get here. They'll have plenty enough to do without bothering about us.'

The Germans let us down. By September they had not come and there was no living like *The Swiss Family Robinson* and no missing school. The map was put away and we resumed our normal lives, driving back to Laragh with Molly, the surviving hens, the bantams and the animals. At school I watched the headmaster moving the flags here and there on the map, listened to Churchill's speeches, and continued to take interest in a possible German invasion. But the Germans proved to be slack.

Some years later, when we were down for the summer, and my mother conceded that by now an invasion was unlikely, we decided to avail ourselves of the hoard. But the map was lost. Had she taken it up to Laragh? She thought it had been left here. But although we searched the house, the folding ship's desk, the cupboards and the loft, filled with sails and shackles and other ship's gear, and even the outdoor Elsan, it was never found.

Meanwhile Jerry and Denis dug up tins which they would bring along to us.

'How very odd!' my mother would say blandly.

They were rusty and dented, their labels had gone. They looked so unattractive, that in most cases we did not even open them. When we did, it was to find sardines and salmon and pilchards past their best – they did not use the words 'sell by' in those days. Some had been eaten away by rust.

'I think you'd better get rid of them. If any of the animals find them, they are bound to get very sick.'

'What a waste!'

During the remainder of the war years petrol ran out and getting to the island became difficult. The first year that we were without motor transport my mother decreed that we should go the two hundred miles from Laragh to Sneem by bicycle. We could not take the dogs, but Prickles had to come. In addition to the pack on my back, my duty was to take my cat – she was always my cat when she became a problem – in a basket strapped behind me.

At Easter we set out, climbing the hill from Laragh to the waterfall at Glenmacnass, walking most of the way, since the bicycles were solidly built without such effete aids as three-speed gears. All the time Prickles grew heavier. Then we made the long downhill spin to Baltinglass and the plains of Kildare.

The journey took three days as we pedalled along eerily empty roads in towns shorn of traffic, where children would be playing in the middle of the main street.

'I think we have had enough, don't you?' my mother would say as we free-wheeled into Naas, or Limerick or Killarney. Prickles was always the first to get attention after our arrival and she had to have her water, milk, and a little liver or chicken from the hotel kitchen. Then we would have our own meal, usually in a dark dining room smelling of cigarette smoke and beer. In Cruises in Limerick the menu was unchanged from the meal I had eaten on my first journey to the island, the one that made me sick. Only at the wonderful Lake Hotel in Killarney did we eat well.

We needed to, since next day we had to tackle the endless climb up to Moll's Gap. Both Phil and I were relieved when at the close of the holiday it was decided that we should return by train.

At the beginning of the summer holidays we once again set out by bicycle and again I was carrying the cat. But before we got to Naas I developed a blister on my backside which made cycling agony.

'It's only a little boil,' Phil said when I took down my trousers. My mother ordered a hot bread poultice from the kitchen. The maid who brought it up had a look. 'Poor crature. Sure its bright red and ready to burst.'

'You'll recover,' Phil said.

The rest of the journey had to be made by bus,

After that, for the rest of the Emergency the entourage travelled down to the island by train. We would stay the night in Fitzwilliam Place before proceeding to the Italian palazzo that was Kingsbridge station. Together with Molly, a couple of dogs, not all of them, and Prickles, forever in her basket – the hens were spared these war-time journeys – we took the Cork train to Limerick Junction, and changed again at Headfort Junction. Those were the days when there was no imported coal and trains were fuelled by wood and turf, which meant that from time to time we would stagger to a stop. We would be left sitting in our carriage looking out at a midland scene of overgrown hedges, pools of water, bog and perhaps a solitary ploughman with seagulls circling his back as they watched every turn of the plough making another brown furrow. He might well be digging up old pasture as part of the government's programme of compulsory tillage. Once the train was refuelled from one of the piles of turf left strategically along the line, we would start again fitfully, clouds of grimy smoke passing our window.

At Headfort we got onto a small local train for the winding branch line down to Kenmare. It was usually empty except for the odd farmer or priest to watch as we ate a gigantic picnic and maybe accept a piece of cake. I have been told that the carriage in which we sat with its fringed purple curtains, dusty bevelled mirrors, bell pulls, Turkey carpets and damp plush sofas and chaise-longues had once been used by Queen Victoria, but more probably the decor was for the benefit of a director of the Great Southern and Western Railway.

The train ambled along, chugging turf smoke out of its little stack, at a speed that seemed to be little more than a brisk walking pace, past Loo Bridge and Kilgarvan into stony green hills down which falls of amber water cascaded. Today the track has vanished under weeds and bracken, the small stone bridges lie broken and water towers resemble decayed Norman castles. The houses in their fuchsia surroundings took on a different look. At the level crossings we would slowly pass a cyclist or two, or a herd of black-faced sheep or a farmer with his stick and belted macintosh and gumboots waiting in the rain beside his sheepdog.

The old terminus at Kenmare, with its single platform, goods yards and solid waiting room, greeted us at the end of the line. In the town people would check their clocks at the sound of the whistle of the arriving train, while the hiss of steam and clank of carriages was the signal for the appearance of the two porters with their trolleys and the station master in his braided uniform.

Outside the station we got our first glimpse of the sea, at the edge of the Kenmare River. Sometimes we would arrive at the end of the fair and walk among lines of bright orange donkey carts, milk churns behind them, cattle, and knots of small men in puckered cloth caps. We would walk beside Jimmy, who came down to greet the train from Kenmare's Great Southern, the sister hotel to the one beside us at Parknasilla; in his bright red porter's jacket he would be wheeling his trolley filled with our suitcases. With the liberated dogs barking and frisking, we would pass the police barracks, Randall's garage and the Lansdowne Arms, once a coaching inn for Victorian tourists on their way to Killarney, to where the grey stone Great Southern stood at the top of the town.

We wandered around the vast empty reception rooms which had turf fires even in midsummer, and views of the estuary and the hills behind. It was difficult for pampered boys to decide which offered more delights, this Great Southern or Killarney's Lake Hotel with its atmosphere of melancholy damp magnificence. Both were luxurious preliminaries to the austerity of the island.

Next morning there was the stop at O'Brien Corkery's store with its long wooden shelves and dark recesses; like Switzers it had a system of overhead wires for receiving change. O'B.C. himself would appear and offer us lemonade and sherry for my mother. Then, among the ropes, anchors, clothes, fishing tackle and old notices for White Star tickets to America, we would go to the counter where John O'Shea the chief shop assistant waited. He would compliment us: 'You've grown very fat,' and take orders for home-cured bacon, country butter and other supplies.

No money changed hands; everything went on the account. The bill would not be sent up to Laragh until the end of the year. We weren't the worst; once, after the war, we saw an American woman come in and pay off the £4. 6s. 6d. which her father had owed when he emigrated thirty years before.

The post car took us to Sneem. We knew every turn and twist of the road that followed the edge of the estuary – the entrance to the O'Mahoney castle, Blackwater Bridge where the *Shira* was laid up, Tahilla and then the drive down to the Oysterbed. On the way down the driver, John Casey could always be relied upon to make any journey interesting. A stretch of the Kenmare estuary would evoke a drowning, a house would be the location for a tale of adultery. And he would point to a cottage tucked away behind a thicket of fuchsia.

'You see that house? Isn't that where the son Jacky cut off

his father's head with an axe and threw the body down the well.'

From the Oysterbed we rowed over to the island, always a quieter place without my father – literally quieter, since there was no fuel to run the boat's engines.

Sometimes my mother invited her friends down, but since wartime transport was so uncertain, it was only occasionally that Win or Hetty or Naomi would make the long journey down to Kerry. Molly was there for company, when she was not cooking mackerel or spying on Jerry and Denis. My mother kept herself busy all day, spending the evenings under the Tilley lamp, playing Monopoly or Hearts with us, or embroidering pieces of tapestry for the dining room chairs at Laragh. She gardened among the fuchsia hedges, azaleas, heathers and gentian blue hydrangeas. The herb and vegetable gardens were tended, and the scent of roses mingled with the tang of seaweed.

We continued to employ Jerry and Denis, who to our eyes were as much fixtures as the growing trees. We knew their families and from time to time we would row over and visit their houses. On those rigidly formal occasions, we would sit by the gleaming black leaded stove beneath the picture of the Sacred Heart and Lizzie or Mary would set out the bone china and the cakes of bread and country butter on the linoleum tablecloth, while Jerry or Denis would watch from the door and smile with approval.

My mother would consult Jerry about the right moment for picking vegetables or killing a hen. If he approved of her orders, he would say, 'I shall be looking into that.' If he had no intention of doing what she asked, he would say, 'Oh, God, I am not so sure.'

The longest argument she had with him was the battle of the Kerry cows. My mother became interested in Kerrys through Belinda the black Dexter, who continued to provide her rich creamy milk. Dexters are like Kerry cows, but their horns curve upwards. Kerry's are just as black, but their horns turn down and they are a little smaller. They have a long history, and descend directly from the herds kept by Celtic farmers.

When my mother broached the idea of buying some Kerrys and taking them up to Laragh, Jerry was horrified. 'Oh, God, no . . . Oh, I wouldn't know about that . . .'

He was not pleased when she persisted and told him that she was bringing down Bill O'Reilly, the Laragh steward, a foreigner from Wicklow. In those days local people did not venture much outside their own areas, unless they were emigrating, and only with the greatest reluctance did O'Reilly agree to journeying to the remote kingdom of Kerry to supervise the buying at Kenmare fair. When he came down with us, by train and post car, the meeting between the taciturn Wicklow man and the foxy Kerry man was sullen.

The idea of sending Kerry cattle to Laragh was broached once again and Jerry said, 'Ah, they'd never do up there!' Wicklow was up north, covered with ice and snow and glaciers. O'Reilly said nothing.

My mother's optimism shone through. After a strained week, which was not helped by Molly keeping an eye on both of them, the men came to surly agreement and went off together in the post car to Kenmare. Convention forbade my mother from accompanying them.

In the cold grey light of early morning, farmers would

have been driving their cattle over the hills to be in time for the tangling. By eight o'clock the wide street lined with carts leading to the Lansdowne Arms and the small cut-stone garda station and miniature prison would be submerged in men and cattle. In one of the numerous pubs, among the fumes of stout and tobacco, where dealers and farmers stood with their pints as the rain poured down outside, O'Reilly and Jerry sealed a rough friendship as both considered each other the proper judges of cattle.

'How did it go?' my mother asked O'Reilly next morning.

As always his face was expressionless. He took out his trusted notebook in which he wrote down all the Laragh expenses – pieces of missing farm machinery, sheep slaughtered, hiring of the reaper and binder, so many poles for fencing, so much turf cut on the bog.

'Six heifers at a good price.'

Nothing more was said, and in due course the pretty bad-tempered black cattle with their proud Celtic pedigree went to Laragh to form a much loved herd of little animals that had the grace and gaiety of fallow deer. Their milk, too creamy for my liking, was splashed into the thinner stuff provided by lesser cows to beef it up, so to speak. And from disparate corners of Ireland the friendship grew between the two men so that some years later Michael, Jerry's son, came and worked in Laragh. Everyone was satisfied.

Phil and I went fishing and sailing with the enthusiasm that we had inherited. It was Phil who organised the laying of long lines and baited lobster pots and night time expeditions after congers, where moonlight and phosphorescence continued to add to the mystery of the hunt.

But sailing took up most of our time. In all weathers we climbed into our little dinghies and raised the sails to move off and explore the complex waters of the Kenmare River. We sailed away in those boats without a care; Bruin was getting old and nowadays he made no effort to leap in beside me. We went out trying to obey the one rule that my father had drummed into us — always respect the wind, tack outwards, and come home down wind.

We could go considerable distances. We sailed to the waters off Parknasilla and Derryquin, a landmark for sailors, the big ruin of the castellated house of the Bland family which had been destroyed in the Troubles. Or we tacked towards Tahilla, around Rossdohan and the house that kept burning down, giving a wide berth to Bullig Point. The other way, if conditions were right we would zig-zag up river, with the home-going salmon, all the way to Sneem on the full tide, returning on the ebb, a thin twisting waterway through stony green hills. The corkscrew course of the river was an obstacle race with hidden rocks and shoals, tidal currents which had to be crossed. No one to watch us, only cattle or the occasional imperious goat looking down at us from the rocks.

We would disembark at the pier and walk up to the small stone bridge that divided Sneem in two; like some great city, each side of Sneem had its own ethos and identity, north and south. The two separate squares, the two churches divided by the stony river and among them a tangle of Kerry names, O'Sheas, O'Caseys, Fitzgeralds and Sullivans, and lurking among them the Christiansons.

It was a grey period when the houses were still grey and only the odd one near the bridge was painted blue.

Nowadays the houses of Sneem are painted every colour of the rainbow, but this practice seems to have begun when General de Gaulle came to stay at Reenafera in the 1950s. The later presence of President O'Dalaigh and the influx of tourists buses and Americans spilling out seeking Aran sweaters and miniature cottages and blackthorn sticks and dishtowels with leprechauns and sayings about 'May the Road Rise Behind You', encouraged the cheerful practice. But there was little colour on the houses in the old days, except for Lena Fitzgerald's Green House, and elsewhere a splash of acid blue, the colour of hydrangeas.

Carcasses of meat were placed on hooks outside the butchers, and on them a crow or two would be pecking away. The odd ass and low backed car driven by men in their caps evoked poverty. Apart from the mail car there was no motor traffic, and the silence was broken only by the chirping swallows and the cries of barefoot children playing on the green where geese wandered.

'And how are you, my little darlings?' Lena Fitzgerald always greeted us as we entered the Green House, with the amazing geranium in the front window, for sweets in glass jars, Bassett's and laces of licorice; a few pennies were enough for them. Across the street was J.J.'s emporium, the largest shop in Sneem with its two hand-cranked petrol pumps outside, and inside the long wooden counter behind which J.J. himself greeted every customer.

'I was only thinking of you the other day. A man I know tells me the first shoals of mackerel have come in.'

The kindly crumpled face with pale blue eyes and ginger moustache, which gave him a faint military air, would break into a smile. There was nothing that J.J. did not know.

Then as the tide turned we would get into our little boats and be carried down the river out to the Oysterbed and over to the island.

There were the other islands to explore. We would go over to neighbouring Garnish and row through the narrow passage whose bottom was strewn with huge scallops. We would land and make our way over the rocks into the jungle they called a garden, with damp ferns, bamboos, rhododendrons which grew higher than if they had stayed home in the Himalayas, and a valley of camellias all thriving among earthy smells of rot and damp. The old gardener gave us a number of tree ferns which we brought back in our dinghies and planted in one of our own island's dark valleys. On other days, followed by porpoises, always with a mackerel line trailing behind each little boat, we would make landfalls on the Pigeon islands or with a good wind and quiet sea reached Inishkeragh, Illaunandan and distant Sherkey.

It was an expression of our wartime sympathies that my mother joined the Dominion Hospitality Trust. This had been set up to entertain soldiers and airmen from Dominion countries who were fighting in the British armed forces and whose homes were far away. Over the course of the war a succession of young men from Canada, South Africa, Australia and New Zealand dropped in on us.

The first were two Australian RAAF pilots, Doug and Frank, who arrived in Dublin wearing their air force blue uniforms. This they were allowed to do, unlike those Irishmen who served in the British forces. On the two occasions when my father had returned from England he had to leave his uniform behind.

It was high summer and we took Doug and Frank down

by train to Illaunslea, where they sailed with us, bending their knees in our little dinghies, trailing fishing lines, while above us squadrons of gannets dive bombed the mackerel, rowed over to the largely deserted Great Southern for a drink, or sat in the sunshine playing the wind-up gramophone.

We had a huge pile of old seventy-eights, records accumulated by my father who, among his other talents, played light jazz on the upright piano that had been part of the Farmhill furnishings. He had a passion for Leslie Hutchinson. In the early 1940s we had practically every song Hutch ever sang, and I wonder how much Doug and Frank and the visitors who followed them cared for a nightclub singer whose heyday had been in the 1930s. Today if I listen to Hutch's deep syrupy voice and his renditions of 'Looking at You' or 'When They Begin the Beguine', I am instantly transported back to hot summer days on the little lawn in front of the island house bordered by flower beds nestling in ribs of rock.

Later on we acquired piles of records of the better known favourites of the forties, Fred Astaire ('The drip drip drip of the rain drops' often so relevant), Fats Waller and Bing Crosby crooning with the Andrews Sisters.

Phil and I sometimes brought down school friends, Among them was Hal, a spotty youth with bright red hair and an infuriating manner of knowing best. When he grew up he became a Cambridge don. One day he took a dislike to my father's collection. 'Ghastly trash!' he said of the songs of Leslie Hutchinson and he threw them out of the window. 'Bilge!' All the beloved warbles of Hutch were destroyed, 'Red Sails in the Sunset', 'I've Got You Under My Skin', 'The

Nearness of You'. Phil and I watched helplessly as one record after another sailed through the air and smashed into pieces. 'Such nonsense!' We spent the rest of the Emergency wondering what my father would say when he returned.

Once I was invited by Radio Eireann to choose three records for a mini version of Roy Plumley's inspiration, *Desert Island Discs*. For copyright reasons islands could not be mentioned, which was a pity, since I know a lot about island-living. I found that no one in the studio had heard of Hutch. After a good deal of searching they dug him from the archives singing 'Smoke Gets in Your Eyes' and exclaimed: 'He's not bad!'

For the many Commonwealth servicemen who stayed at Laragh and came to the island after Doug and Frank, those days in Kerry provided a strange serene break from a war which would claim the lives of a number of them. For them the weather was good ('What raindrops?') and the sun shone; the water of the Kenmare River was blue as sapphire. The letters they wrote to my mother indicated that they had experienced the exhilaration that the island gave to so many who went there.

They made us feel closer to what was taking place in the world outside neutral Ireland, and brought a whiff of excitement into our lives. We felt deeply envious of them. At the most they were half a dozen years older than the schoolboys that we were, but the years and experience made a chasm between us. They rarely talked of their experiences and when we said goodbye and they returned to fight in the air or on the ground, it was on the supposition that we would not see them again.

There has been one exception. A few years ago I received

a letter from a former airman, now living in Sydney, who was visiting Ireland for the first time since 1943.

Dear Peter, I heard you were living in Dublin and I remembered the wonderful time I had with you all. Your mum was a real sweetheart, and I can't tell you how much it meant to me and the rest of us, those few weeks at Laragh and Illaunslea. I hope you still have the island . . .

Later he came to Dublin and we met up; the blond young pilot who had flown bombers over Germany had changed to a white-haired doctor. His memories of his brief stay in Ireland over half a century ago were lyrical, all but one moment at Laragh.

Your mum said in that high voice of hers, 'Bruce, why don't you go for a swim in the lake? One of the boys will lend you a bathing suit.' So I did, and I climbed up to the top of the diving platform and dived in. Oh, Christ, I have never forgotten how cold that water was.

11

My Uncles

MY FATHER'S TWO brothers, Uncle Paddy and Uncle Becher, had houses in the vicinity of Dublin. Brooklawn, belonging to Uncle Becher, was to the west of the city, a Georgian house made elegant by a small ballroom, a drawing room with a bow-fronted window overlooking the Liffey, and a divided staircase rising like a soufflé towards the sky. It was filled with pictures, among them a mystical Jack Yeats, of a horse walking through a bluish landscape, bought from the artist half a century before his paintings became millionaires' trophies.

Uncle Becher's wife, Aunt Sammy, coveted other pictures by Yeats. Around 1943 she saw in the window of Victor Waddington's art gallery in Dublin three of his outstanding paintings – *The Island Funeral*, *Communicating with Prisoners*, and the haunting *Bachelor's Walk, in Memory*, showing a flower girl dropping a carnation on the place where a rebel soldier had died. They were all priced at thirty pounds. After much thought she decided that it would be wrong to spend money in wartime on such luxuries. The painting of the flower girl was bought by Lady Dunsany. Many years later it was stolen from the hall of Dunsany Castle, and to this day has not been recovered.

Uncle Becher was a perfectionist, and like his brothers,

possessed of nervous energy. Whether making a fly for trout fishing, lecturing to some archaeological association, designing a wrought-iron gate or laying out a walled garden, he brought to the task the same dedication as he did to his profession which was that of an ophthalmologist.

Like my father, Uncle Becher went off to war and was away for years. He went to India to look after soldiers' eyes. He adored India and was impressed by the Hindu religion and way of life, which was unusual for those times. Many of his contemporaries found the Hindu religion baffling or disgusting. He brought back a number of exquisite pieces of sculpture which adorned Brooklawn, a small shrine under the beech trees near the back yard, and the sacred bull and elephant at the entrance to the walled garden. I still have a treasured Indian Mogul painting that he gave me.

Uncle Paddy, the only brother to stay at home, was a railway engineer who had begun his career repairing railway bridges blown up by Republicans during the Civil War. He became chief engineer of CIE, the national transport company, and throughout the Emergency helped to keep the trains running on turf and wood.

He had other duties and interests. He dealt with the nagging demands of Lady Maffey at Farmhill. He was a partner in the Country Shop set up by Muriel Gahan to provide an outlet for selling rugs and Aran sweaters and suchlike, made by country women. He served on various hospital boards and, although his brothers were both doctors, did not care for medical men.

'Leeches!'

He disliked other lowly types like Eamon de Valera, solicitors and accountants, people who smoked, and people who played golf. He hated my father's golf courses, a waste of good land.

He was involved in all sorts of unusual charity work, including the creation of a self-help organisation which he called the Mount Street Club – an ironic contrast to the Kildare Street Club. Founded in the 1930s when unemployment was at its peak, the Mount Street Club had its own internal economy, in which food and clothing were offered in exchange for tallies awarded for work on the farm which was purchased at Lucan. Any unemployed man could enrol and exchange the tallies he earned for the product of other men's work – he could get potatoes and vegetables, or his clothes made or mended by the resident tailor or his boots repaired by the cobbler. Regarded as an eccentric philanthropic oddity, the Club worked very well, its philosophy bearing some resemblance to that of Robert Owen and the community at Lanark, although Uncle Paddy knew nothing about Owen. He and a couple of friends thought up the idea themselves.

Uncle Paddy and Aunt Grace lived in Vallombrosa, a grey gabled house outside Bray surrounded by trees overlooking the Sugarloaf Mountain. The interior was filled with much of the Brisbania from Farmhill, as well as the moustached portraits of Uncle Bris and Uncle Phil. However there were better pictures in the house than those daubs by journeymen artists. Aunt Grace was a niece of William Orpen, and when he died she and her five sisters were each bequeathed one of his paintings. Aunt Grace's choice was a portrait of a girl dressed in black, wearing a black bandeau, who we were told was a barmaid, not Uncle Paddy's preferred subject. She was beautiful, and she was dying – a few months after the portrait was completed she was dead of TB. Uncle Paddy bought a companion to this picture, a portrait of a pretty nun who, although he did not know it, was William Orpen's mistress dressed up. He paid a hundred pounds for it, and later could never believe that the prices of Orpen's pictures had gone up. 'It's only worth a hundred pounds!' he would persist in saying, on hearing of some sale of an Orpen for a six-figure sum.

Like my father, Uncle Paddy practised self-sufficiency. They both had an obsession with home-produced electricity, and at Vallombrosa a water turbine worked to some extent. Many evenings were lit by dim flickering light bulbs, which came on after a ceremony with levers and switches from a huge switchboard. Whatever the hour, however dark it was and however much it was raining, failure of the turbine was followed by a trip by torchlight down to the river to see why it was misbehaving.

Two walled gardens had an abundance of utilitarian vegetables, cabbages and Brussels sprouts and endless cut-and-come again spinach. I do not think many people grew courgettes in those days, but Uncle Paddy disapproved of them as pansy marrows. The marrows he grew were as big as barrage balloons. He disapproved of new potatoes, which he considered should be left to grow bigger; the potatoes at Vallombrosa were eaten mature, after thick black muddy skins had been peeled off and big holes were pierced in their sides to get rid of big black eyes.

Chickens were kept in an amazing chicken run whose waving roof line, which would not have been out of place in Barcelona, had been constructed by throwing concrete over fence wire. It was huge and fox-proof, and the red hens inside had a good life with plenty of room to move about and lay and lay. Like the potatoes and marrows, Uncle Paddy let them grow to maturity and old age before they were dispatched and boiled for a long time; there was usually a residue of old feathers on their legs.

In spring the lines of apple trees formed a pink and white forest. In autumn every year the numerous acres of apple trees were the target of raids by the boys of Bray. Alleys of raspberries were flecked red in July. Nothing could be more dazzling than the pear orchard, either during the brief staggered period of spring blossom, or in autumn when the fruits of the different species ripened, their colours confined to a narrow gleaming spectrum of green and gold and pale rose, their drooping sack shapes all a little different. The trees hung with treasures, early Jaguelle, shining green Concorde, golden Gorham, Conference cut open and eaten with a spoon like an avocado, Doyenne du Comice touched with crimson, its autumn leaves a fiery red and late Josephine de Malines.

The house was filled with books. There was very little fiction since Uncle Paddy had no time for it. ('What about *War and Peace*, Uncle Pad?' 'Waste of time.') The exceptions were the works of P.G. Wodehouse of which he had a full collection. The Herbert Jenkins titles stood in a neat line on a special shelf in the study – *Money for Nothing*, *A Damsel in Distress*, *Summer Lightening*, *Uncle Fred in the Springtime*, and even those stories devoted to despised golf, like *The Clicking of Cuthbert* and *The Heart of a Goof*. They had a formative effect on Uncle Paddy's vocabulary and speech patterns. ('My sainted aunt!' 'My hat!')

Other books had to be informative or instructive. Plenty

of history, manuals on turbines and chicken diseases, typed family reminiscences and photograph albums filled with pictures of people in Edwardian clothes and earlier ones with brass clasps, brown Victorian portraits, carefully labelled and identified – Uniacke Redmond, Col. John Limerick, Isabelle Chavasse, all given a kind of immortality.

Gadgets made life simpler, like the wheel that blew the damp turf on the drawing room fire or the silver-plated egg boiler, turned black by methylated spirits. In the workshop, located in the conservatory, there was always something waiting to be mended, home-made skis or the dismantled engine of a car. Carpenter's tools mingled with tin boxes of screws and nails and ancient guns lying among some Indian swords and a broken harem screen. A sword from the ancestor who had fought at Balaclava lay beside a huge carpet bag for cricket bats that had been taken to India by Uncle Phil; later I took it to Afghanistan. Next door a clutch of chickens could usually be heard cheeping in their incubator. Dark rooms in the back had their own particular clutter – one was full of hundreds of religious tomes and books of sermons which had belonged to my grandfather, another had cardboard boxes filled with broken china waiting to be stuck with Seccotine (no time!) and empty china jars which once contained Gentleman's Relish. (They'll come in useful!)

While my father was away Uncle Paddy would occasionally come down to Laragh to see how we were getting on. He would motor over the hills from Bray, a cloud of coke fumes engulfing his specially adapted car, bringing some guns and Maffey. First of all there would be a painful session with my mother and Major Mandeville looking at accounts.

Then we would set out with the guns. The Bog Meadow was a good place for snipe and there was the odd pheasant or grouse. Neither Phil nor I were any good at this gentlemanly pursuit, but Uncle Paddy would regularly lift his gun in the air and kill a pheasant, or follow the zig-zag flight of a snipe for Maffey to bring in the pathetic bunch of feathers. But it was mostly rabbits that we shot at, aiming and hearing the squeal.

'Fetch, fetch!' And, waving his tail, Maffey would retrieve one more for Molly's pies or for the hungry Welsh.

Uncle Paddy's car was a Terroplane, a large open American vehicle in the boot of which he had contrived to fit a coke burning stove on which it ran in lieu of petrol. It looked fragile and Heath Robinsonian, with its backside taken up by a boiler and numerous tubes attached to a pump and a blower. The pieces of carbon inside the boiler were lit by a cloth pushed into one of the tubes and ignited.

'I think that should be all right,' he would shout as the furnace behind him roared like a lion, and off we would go for a drive. I would be in the back seat and if the wind was in the wrong direction would receive fumes of carbon monoxide. It was worse than driving with my father, and my uncle was just as callous.

My mother had spent much of her childhood in the North of Ireland at a house named Willsboro and had imbibed the atmosphere arising from Protestant servants and listening to the Lambeg drums on hot summer nights. Occasionally she would entertain us with those stories that contributed to the Protestant myth. We were told of King William's troops linking arms and stepping into the shallow waters of the Boyne, while fifes and drums played

'Lillibullero'. We might have little knowledge of the history of the country to which we belonged, but we knew all about the villain Lundy, the brave Apprentice Boys, and the starving citizens of Londonderry buying a dog's head at 2s. 6d., a cat at 4s. 6d. and rats at a shilling each – they could not have been worse to eat than rabbits.

In the Christmas holidays of the fourth year of the Emergency, my mother had enough of wind and rain and solitude, and proposed a visit to her Uncle Jack, a crotchety old man who lived in Willsboro.

'To the North?' A country at war.

The train from Amiens Street Station, fuelled like all the rest with wood and turf, went north beside the sea at the same stuttering pace as the train that took us down to Limerick Junction. When we crossed the Boyne my mother told us, a little sheepishly, how in the old days her family seated in their carriage used to rise to their feet as the train thundered over the river and remember King William and his victory.

At the border a small blue-coated custom official with a drooping moustache asked us if we had anything to declare. We were aware that smuggling didn't take place in trains to any extent, but outside in the damp green country where cattle were driven across the border, cigarettes, petrol and guns were being shifted and whiskey was carried over in coffins at the heart of make-believe funeral cortèges.

Gradually as we slowly steamed into Northern Ireland there were signs that we had left Eire behind.

'Look how neat everything is,' my mother said.

We noticed trimmed hedges and wider roads with many more cars and lorries, which we knew were fuelled by brave tankers dodging Nazi U-boats. At Newry a soldier came into our carriage with his knapsack and spoke broad Cockney. Before we arrived at the small red brick terraces of Portadown we went to the lavatory; underneath the notice requesting passengers not to pull the chain when the train was in the station, someone had written, 'except at Portadown'.

After that we counted Union Jacks fluttering from every church tower, more interesting than counting white horses. We were perfectly familiar with Union Jacks. At Baymount every year on sports day the school always flew one until the local guard cycled up the avenue and told the Headmaster to take it down. The same thing happened at Castle Park.

It was dark when we drew into Belfast and the city was dark with blackout, the shops were sandbagged and the streets lacked Christmas decorations. Only yesterday we had been in the bright lights of O'Connell Street. Next morning we could see the damage from the devastating raid that had flattened the city. Apart from Liverpool and London, no city in the British Isles had suffered so many casualties in one night.

Hundreds of service people walked the ruined streets, Yanks, black and white, chewing gum, airmen, navy officers and perky Wrens. We nudged each other and whispered that the Belfast girls with their lipsticks and tight skirts were more sexy than anyone in Dublin. Did one of them flash a smile at us? Probably not.

We took the train to the place my mother firmly called Londonderry, where we called in on some elderly cousins who lived in red brick Victorian house behind impenetrable laurels.

'Joyce – its been so long . . .' Thirty years had passed since my mother had seen Cousin Laura and Cousin Elizabeth, now in their nineties. Their courtly voices were very unlike the gruff northern accents we had been listening to since we crossed the border.

We were led through the main hall, which was lined with glass cases full of stuffed animals and birds, mostly mouldy and decayed. Some of the glass was cracked. The alligator, out of whose mouth appeared the backside and hind legs of its stuffed prey, had lost some of its skin. A spider monkey lacked a leg. The toucans and parrots were tousled and dusty.

Over tea the talk was of relations.

'Poor pet, completely paralyzed . . .'

'Out in Bulawayo . . . we haven't heard from him for years . . .'

'He died just before the war . . .'

'Alfred was before your time, my dear. He went off to the orange groves of Florida . . .'

Before we left Cousin Laura asked, 'My dears, would you like me to play you a hymn?'

The organ, whose decorated pipes rose in tiers towards the ceiling, stood at the back of the hall beyond the glass cases.

Cousin Elizabeth said, 'We don't play often nowadays. Some notes aren't quite what they should be and we can't get a man to repair it.'

But Cousin Laura persisted and we listened to 'All Things Bright and Beautiful' which sounded like a dirge. Mrs Alexander, who wrote it, came from these parts.

'Another?' And we listened to 'Rock of Ages' and all its Freudian imagery.

'Things are so different nowadays,' Cousin Elizabeth said

to my mother. 'Do you remember your grandmother playing the harmonium in Faughanvale? She was a true musician, playing every Sunday and teaching that wonderful choir.'

'Such voices! Trebles, seconds, tenor and bass . . .'

'Oh, God,' Phil said as we drove away, 'it was worse than having tea with Mrs Penrose.'

The taxi took us on to Eglington, a trim village on the shores of Lough Foyle founded by some London Livery Company, where there was a cricket ground and a number of trees planted to commemorate the coronations of English kings and queens. Beyond the mock Tudor pub we entered the gates of Willsboro flanked by a crested lodge and a long winding avenue. Oddly there was something suitably Dutch in feeling in that landscape, flat as a board. But then you looked across Lough Foyle to where the Donegal mountains rose up.

Uncle Jack lived alone in the rambling old house, a long two-storey building with Venetian shutters framing the lines of windows. Every room was crowded with furniture and paintings and the servants were all Protestant. A forlorn old-fashioned lunch was served in the dining room lined with portraits of ancestors, where we were hidden from one another by the vastness of the silver epergne in the centre of the table. Afterwards we retired to the dark study where the shutters were closed and the tiny fire was more ornamental than warm. Uncle Jack brought out a pair of duelling pistols from a green baize box and allowed us to point them at each other.

My mother said, 'What happened to the parrot?'

'Oh, she did not live for long after Hatta went.' My mother's Great Aunt Hatta had died, aged a hundred and seven, and the parrot was supposed to have been as old as she was.

For the rest of the day we trailed around the estate after Uncle Jack. He pointed out the small railway station which had once been for the exclusive use of the family. Behind the clock tower were the red brick walls of an immense garden which had once grown strawberries, black cherries and other produce which my mother could remember being tended by hordes of gardeners. Huge greenhouses were choked with briars. The croquet lawn, where my mother had played, was covered in weeds and the tennis courts were obliterated. Much of the woodlands had been cut down.

This was the sort of ruin associated with the ruined demesnes familiar to us in the South of Ireland, not with the neat and tidy north. My great uncle seemed unmoved by the sepulchre in which he lived. We were not sorry to leave the gloom of Willsboro and return to the South by Lough Erne, where even the sight of some flying boats failed to cheer us, because they reminded us that our cousin, Humphry, had been killed in one. In the dim December twilight we were bitterly disappointed to find that in the midst of a country gallantly at war, our own relations were as nutty as our neighbours in Laragh.

My mother kept her thoughts to herself. I wonder if she pondered that the society to which she was linked, with its lofty bigotry, had become as isolated in the North of Ireland as it was in the South? It was a voluntary alienation that threatened to descend below eccentricity to madness. And perhaps my father's island in Kerry was a symbol of the desire to be alone and aloof, although it is going too far to equate his love for the island with the monks of Skellig Michael contemplating the trackless sea.

Very soon after our visit Uncle Jack died and the house and contents were sold. In due course the house became a ruin.

Meanwhile my father was enjoying his life as a soldier which he spent setting up and inspecting hospitals in Africa and the Middle East. When he returned after the war he edited his diary, which covered four years, and numerous countries, and had it typed out. The hefty document has survived, filled with files, indexes, maps, photographs, illustrations, magazine articles, tourist brochures, and lists of ancient kings and dynasties. The photographs cover a range of interests from groups of colleagues, to the six wives of a Nigerian chieftain, to the Pyramids, to a man dying of smallpox in Kanu.

During the time he was away he was seldom far from boats. In Alexandria he stayed at the Royal Egyptian Yacht Club and hired a twenty-foot sailing boat in which he explored the harbour, dodging and gybing round the buoys and vessels. 'Ships crowded the harbour – dozens of trading schooners, very short with high sides . . . Italian cruisers and destroyers, enormous aircraft carriers, naval launches and speed boats racing everywhere.'

On the Suez Canal he noted the grace and efficiency of Nile barges:

Although these large craft have the peculiar flat up-turned bows, they get along at a surprising speed. If they are going at all close-hauled they proceed half sideways to allow for their leeway, but if the wind is anyway free they turn up a cheery foam across the bows and get along in great style. Long lines of them coming one after the other are beautiful as they heel slightly to the strong breeze.

At the entrance to Lake Tinsah he saw King Farouk's steam yacht ('very old-fashioned') and later in Iran inspected the yacht abandoned by exiled Reza Shah. ('Her decking is thin and cheap, her door narrow, ceiling very low, no good panelling . . . no comfortable salon or dining room . . . Her engines are permanently dead.')

In Iraq he went on a moonlight picnic. He and his friends were rowed gently down the Euphrates in two boats, with a number of servants, including a cook, and six large live fish towed behind them for their dinner. ('Baghdad salmon must be eaten absolutely fresh.')

The riverside cafes are crowded with Arabs sitting on wooden benches at tables and playing dominoes or chess. From each is heard that variety of rhythmic nasal noise regarded as beautiful singing. Out here on the water . . . drinks in ice, nuts and fruit are provided in profusion . . . We lie back on our cushions and the full moon lights up the towers and minarets of the town. All the squalor and dirt, the smells, the flies, the crowded hustling humanity, the stream of huge cars of the rich Arabs and the taxis all endlessly blowing their horns, the laden donkeys . . . the camels, the water buffaloes . . . are all miles away, only the beauty of the town reaches us here.

They anchored at an island where a feast was prepared by the servants and the salmon were eaten. After their meal the boats were dragged upstream by the boatmen paddling near the shore.

It is a gentle progress and I think of old Nebuchadnezzar running down the Euphrates so easily from Babylon to his palace at Ur, and the long pull back again.

He wrote incessantly about archaeology, his new passion. 'Ur of the Chaldees, the birthplace of the Patriarch Abraham, the cradle of civilisation' was only one of the ancient sites he visited during his tour of the Middle East. Observations at Babylon, Nimrod, Nineveh, Baalbeck, and at the famous Egyptian sites, were recorded:

It is undoubtedly a Hittite carving of 664 to 500 BC . . . The carving shows King Kurs . . . on his left hand stands Metra, the Sun God, and on his right hand Anaita, the Babylon goddess of fertility. This shows that in AD 600 they were still worshipping Babylonian gods.

The diary is filled with observations of people he worked with or met on his travels. Some are enthusiastically favourable, like his encounter with a Dutch priest, one of the greatest authorities on Persian history '. . . a first class scholar, delightful manners, and he made us welcome.'

But his opinions of others were caustic. He had no time for missionaries.

Mrs Gurney has had typhoid and diphtheria . . . and so little does she realise the dangers that she does 'not believe in boiling water before she drinks it'. I cannot find much sympathy, neither do I think it is a noble spirit that leads them to take such unnecessary risks in order to spread the Gospel.

His most acid comments were reserved for those he worked with. A commanding officer of one hospital was dismissed as 'an RAMC regular who is selfish and not fit to command'; another 'a typical Aberdeen Scot who does not know how bad a surgeon he is, and will never be able to learn'.

Among his conclusions:

the English should remember that they're extremely bad at making friends with Natives of other countries, they do not realise this enough, and many go about the world believing they are popular while actually their air of superiority, self satisfaction and bored intelligence has quite the opposite effect.

I found the idea of my father as a closet Irish nationalist strangely endearing.

But other nationalities also provoked scorn.

The wretched Indian surgeons, majors and lieutenant-colonels who get infinitely more than their corresponding ranks in the British army, are dangerous, incompetent and without judgment.

Throughout the war he still found time to dream about the island. Hardly a letter came from him to my mother without some reference to that small exposed teardrop in the Kenmare River. Were the paths being kept properly cleared? Remember to use potassium chloride on the tennis court to keep down weeds. What about the boats? The *Kingfisher*, hauled up on its trolley below the suspension bridge must have its engine regularly serviced. The *Shira* at Blackwater Bridge must be checked, so must the nets and fishing gear. He made plans for the swimming pool and for planting new wind breaks. He might be going down the Tigris, but for five years he never stopped thinking of the sea-washed rocks of Illaunslea.

At last the war was over and it was time to return to Ireland. 'Goodbye, Baghdad, goodbye, Agri Quf – goodbye, old desert – the land of Rafidhain – the twin rivers I have flown over so often.' He noted that the two young pilots who flew the great flying boat called *Champion*, in which he was a passenger, were only a little older than his sons.

Soon after he arrived back he presented us with a scrapbook.

'I want you to study this very carefully. And never forget what has happened.'

The scrapbook consisted of news cuttings and pictures of German concentration camps. He had found time to assemble it between his official duties, his travels, his days of relaxation, his visits to archaeological sites and keeping his diary. Later I mentioned it to a friend whose father had also compiled a scrapbook – of Allied atrocities, which was also, alas, pretty full with its details of carpet bombings, revenge killings and reports on Dresden and Hiroshima.

I remember the strain of my father's return and our shyness. He had been away for too long and love had withered. The word 'daddy' was strange on our lips. Long before the wartime separation the *cordon sanitaire* that surrounded children like us and divided us from our parents had kept him at a distance. The years away had brought us closer to our mother, and we loved her humour and her gallant resilience to loneliness. The peaceful existence we had evolved with her was at an end. We hardly knew this man with grey hair who had suddenly barged into our lives. He had left behind two small boys and when he came back they had become moody teenagers who found him a stranger. It was a common enough tragedy of the time.

12

Who Is the Baby in the Pram?

ALMOST THE FIRST thing my father did after returning from the war was to go down to the island.

Our years of quiet ended abruptly. Once again large parties of people were invited down and more cars filled with friends and relations arrived on the Oysterbed Pier, blew their horns and waited for a boat to take them across. Once again they were put to work, clearing trees and laying long lines. There was the old animation and excitement, and new plans for sailing parties, fishing parties and swimming parties.

He continued the programme of improvements that he had planned before he left. It was as if he had never gone away. He had a substantial garage built on the mainland, big enough for a couple of cars and a boat or two; after the island was sold someone easily turned it into a comfortable holiday home. For a time the island itself continued to ring with sounds of dynamite clearing the rocks for the swimming pool. But his enthusiasm for this waned; after swimming in the Middle East he found the sea water that was supposed to fill up the pool with each tide was too cold for enjoyment, and the pool was never finished. The rest of us continued to swim and dive off the rocks at the west end of the island. What was this myth about the warm waters of the Gulf Stream?

Around us in Kerry and in other parts of Ireland an odd temporary change was taking place. This was what became known as the Retreat from Moscow. Those who wished to flee from Clement Attlee's Britain dominated by new radical social ideas and high taxation were attracted to Ireland where they perceived that conservative values still reigned, food was not rationed and servants were plentiful. Ironically, at the same time during those bitter post-war years thousands of Irishmen were flocking to England in search of work.

Kerry particularly attracted those who took part in the Retreat. They settled around the Kenmare River and not only were most of them rich, but they tended to belong to another generation of majors and colonels, as if there were not enough from the old days and the first war.

We kept a close eye on them.

'Bad form using their wartime ranks!'

Six years of war and conscription had not diminished British military snobberies. People would still talk with contempt in their voices about poor old so-and-so who had risen from the ranks. Or some other poor so-and-so, who thought he'd get into a guard's regiment and had ended up in the Signals. The Signals!

Large new houses sprang up all over Kerry or old ones were converted and made luxurious; some had central heating. Across the bay from us a brigadier was building a particularly lavish mansion. From our island a jeering party would sail out and watch its construction. Binoculars would be passed around.

'Too big.'

'Too ostentatious.'

'That fat untidy woman must be his wife.'

'How did he get planning permission?'

'Palms were greased, of course.'

The brigadier brought a large motor yacht over from Southampton which he sailed in what my father considered were our own private waters. He watched critically through the binoculars tut-tutting at some nautical indiscretion as the yacht shot towards Garnish.

'Fancy flying the White Ensign – doesn't know a thing about yachts.'

In Sneem Winnie Hurley smiled at the English strangers coming in and buying their whiskey. 'They will not be here long,' she said. And she was proved right. A few years later the Labour Party was defeated and nearly all of them went back to England. No one wanted their smart houses and most proved unsaleable. The brigadier took off the roof of his new house in order to avoid paying rates.

Perhaps the lavish expenditure of the newcomers inspired my father to install a few luxuries. Instead of the dry larder we now had a Calor gas fridge, and the Tilley and oil lamps were supplemented by Calor gas. But the spartan Elsans were not replaced, and smells of disinfectant contested the scent of fish and the turf fire from the little stove in the sitting room.

While we had massive boats like the *Kingfisher*, and the *Shira* moored in the bay in all their beauty and extravagance, the regular ferries to and from the island and the Oysterbed continued in a series of ancient rowing boats to which outboard engines were attached. Our new neighbours had inboard engines which started at the touch of a button, while we struggled with Johnsons and Seagulls, temperamental as debutantes. Too often when you pulled at the rope nothing happened and the boat would start drifting sideways towards rocks.

Elsewhere there were changes in our lives. On his return from the Middle East my father took one look at Laragh.

'We can't go on living here.'

The shock of seeing those windy Wicklow acres galvanised him. That he had lost his enthusiasm for them was hardly surprising, since his financial losses were horrendous. He had put huge sums of money into the restoration of the house and farm and the building up of the hotel, but his investment had no opportunity to bring in any dividends. For six years the hotel had been empty for ten months of each year. All those years hotel staff and farm workers had to be paid, and even if they received thirty shillings a week and a pair of boots at Christmas, the wages bill was large.

The idea of selling up was a good excuse for a farewell party for all his friends. It was wonderful, almost the best he ever gave, as memorable as the inaugural party on Illaunslea in 1935. I was not there for it, but for many years heard details of how for three days and nights he entertained around a hundred people at the hotel on a princely scale. He offered them all the facilities for which the usual hotel guests paid money, and deliriously they indulged in tennis, golf, and riding. In the evenings, they put on evening clothes and after a succession of banquets danced to a good band, specially hired. Laragh went out in a festival of light.

The place was put up for auction. Among those who came

to view it was Archbishop McQuaid, who may have had some plans of turning it into a religious house. When he came down in his black chauffeur-driven Citroën and my mother entertained him to tea, we had visions of sandalled monks in brown robes hoeing and raking. Or perhaps nuns in white wimples? All the workers on the estate queued up to be presented to the feared and venerated Archbishop and knelt to kiss his ring.

On the day of the auction we trooped into the office of the Dublin auctioneers where we were taken to the back room, haunted by lost hopes, whose walls were covered with photographs of large houses successfully sold mainly to English people taking part in the Retreat from Moscow.

We drank tea and ate Marietta biscuits in silence while the hour came and went. There was a sense of unease as we waited in the belief that the auction was taking place downstairs in a room that was full of people who had come out of curiosity. The idea was that Mr Smith, the auctioneer, would come up bearing news of the top bid and my parents would discuss it.

The door creaked open and Mr Smith's hesitant face appeared.

'I'm afraid there were no bids.'

'None?'

'None.'

Since 1935 my father had poured money, energy and ideas into transforming a derelict estate into a promising and lucrative enterprise. And now no one wanted it, not the Archbishop, nor anyone else. Perhaps the ghost of Mr Booth, emanating depression, discouraged those who drove the long miles to view the place. It remained on our hands for several years until it was privately sold to an English syndicate at a huge loss. My father never mentioned the subject of Laragh again to us.

In the course of time the main house burnt down, and local rumour suggested that the fire was deliberately started to gain insurance money. Some of the granite stones were used to build the new bridge at Laragh village. The only part to survive the fire was Michael Scott's' new ballroom and, like the garage beside the Oysterbed, that was big enough to be turned into a comfortable house.

Today a German lives there, and I went to visit him.

He said, 'I cannot understand why there should be so much sand in the fields when I am ploughing.'

I could explain. When Laragh was finally disposed of, no one wanted a golf course, let alone two. When the green sward, which had survived wartime regulations about tillage, was finally ploughed up, there were always square patches in any crop planted there that did not do well. The seed for the German's oats had been sown, not exactly on stony ground, but on the sand where the greens and bunkers were laid out, leaving traces that would have deceived a future archaeologist.

Where were we going to live? My father was determined to get away from the hotel and the farm and the whole white elephant. He wanted to move nearer to Dublin and nearer to his brothers. In spite of their constant expressions of disapproval about each other's activities, they were all very fond of each other.

There was plenty of choice among big houses rejected by the Retreat people, but most houses on offer were too large or too cold for post-war needs. The servant shortage terrified the affluent classes. Young women did not want to be domestic servants any more and there was a general dread of having to do one's own washing up. In those days house property was not considered an asset but a liability, a nightmare of rates and roofs.

Among the houses we looked at was Lucan House, a magnificent Palladian mansion overlooking the Liffey. But the grand interior, full of marble columns and neoclassical decoration on walls and ceilings, much admired by Georgian purists, was much too sugary for my father's taste. In addition, the place was well maintained which he considered a serious drawback. There was nothing to improve or change. So Lucan was bought by the Italian government and became the Italian embassy.

Eventually he acquired a smaller house, only half a mile from Vallombrosa where Uncle Paddy lived, with a similar view of the Sugarloaf. The grounds covering fifty acres and the River Dargle ran out of the Dargle Glen through them – very suitable for the inevitable dynamo which would provide electricity – and the whole place needed immediate attention.

St Valery was a substantial villa built in the style of the Morrison dynasty of architects who had an influence on gentlemen of moderate means. In 1790 a small house at the entrance to the Dargle Glen had been transformed by an invalid gentleman named Joseph Walker, who used his talents as amateur architect, giving his house a tower and an air of Gothic romance. The tall sunlit rooms, some oval with bow-fronted windows, were all different and all beautiful. Outside he planted trees, including a couple of cedars which had grown huge by the time we arrived, and diverted the river to become a lake full of swans. The lake had gone and instead we had a swampy tennis court in its place.

Mr Walker was 'that elegant scholar, that man of refined classical taste' in the opinion of Anne Plumptre who stayed with him for five days at 'a sweet spot, but it stands in a country where every spot is sweet.' Like my father, he liked company and encouraged visitors like Miss Plumptre, who were doing the tourist round of Wicklow, to call in. Another was Sir John Carr who in 1805 described Mr Walker as an invalid

> blessed with a variety of knowledge ancient and modern, a long residence in Italy, a correspondence with the most distinguished literary men of the age . . . a felicity of temper and a resignation to the hand of heaven.

When Sir Walter Scott visited St Valery in 1825 Mr Walker was dead and a surgeon named Philip Crampton lived there. Crampton was interested in natural history and a hippopotamus skull from his collection still lay on a table under the balcony beneath the drawing room window. Until the 1960s a strange little fountain surrounded by bronze reeds and birds stood in his memory in College Street in Dublin. After Crampton there had been various owners until we bought the house from an obscure Protestant sect; when we first came up to inspect it, psalms and hymns could be heard coming out of the long windows of the drawing room.

My father furnished the place with our effects brought along from Laragh. Much had been inherited, like the upright piano on which he occasionally played a light piece of jazz before going off to do something more important.

When the contents of Farmhill were divided up between the brothers, Uncle Becher chose the few things that were beautiful, like the *famille rose* plates, while Uncle Paddy ended up with much of the Brisbania. My father was happy with the stuffed heads, antlers and horns of animals shot by Uncle Phil. Buffalo and sambur and the rare *ovis poli* with big curved horns, which had adorned the damp walls of Laragh, found congenial new lookouts.

From Russia, via my grandfather's Uncle Paddy, so named because he was the only Irish officer in his unit of the Rifle Brigade, came a number of Minié balls, welded together, turned into inkwells and labelled in Cyrillic lettering *Sevastopol*. Perhaps the swords displayed in sunbursts came from this Uncle Paddy, veteran of the Crimean War. From Uncle Bris came a Japanese hara-kiri sword accompanied by a special little sword which the honourable suicide was supposed to use at the beginning of the proceedings to slice a small preliminary wound. The ivory scenes of torture beguiled passers-by from their display cabinet.

In addition to what he had inherited, my father had accumulated a number of things that reflected his personal preferences. There was room in the hallway of St Valery for the antlers from two great Irish elks from Kilkenny Castle which he had bought at an auction in 1935 when the Duke of Ormond sold up – they dwarfed any trophy of Uncle Phil's. Pikes and spears were acquired at the same auction. Some ship's steering wheels were converted into lights and the hall was dominated by a line of matching bronze bells, each inscribed *Erin Go Bragh*. Model ships included a large Chinese junk and a kayak from the people we used to call Eskimos but are now know as Innuit. Over the years my father had acquired a long wooden ram for charging cannon used at the siege of Paris, Persian miniatures bought in Iran, ancient Egyptian scarabs and ushpati, some blue glazed tiles from Tamberlaine's tomb in Samarkand and the pair of so-called Armada cannon bought at Colonel Hartley's auction in Kerry.

My mother made her contribution, some pieces of furniture inherited from Willsboro and effects from judges, ambassadors and missionaries who were among her forebears. From her family came one of Tipoo's many swords acquired after Seringapatam and scrolls from grateful Chinese merchants praising a forebear named William Phillips who was Governor of Prince Edward Island, later called Penang.

> With reverence we reflect, that ever since you, our virtuous king and ruler, gloriously received the exalted decree – the justice and fidelity of your administration have spread the fame of your pure virtue to all parts; and your tenderness towards the people who have been cherished as your children . . .
>
> Your intelligence has surpassed in rightness the sun and the moon. Your beneficence has emulated the heavens and the earth. Your integrity, clear as the gem, and translucent as the ice, has caused us to admire the purity of the autumnal stream, unsullied by the dust of earth . . .

And so on and so forth.

William Phillips was tight-lipped as any Englishman abroad. 'My Chinese pundit admired the Parchment Address very much. He chaunted over the periods with great satisfaction when I showed him the composition.'

My mother's brother, Uncle Will, inherited many of these fulsome addresses written on parchment and found a use for them – he turned them into lampshades.

William Phillips' descendants became respected members of the establishment, clergymen, a Commissioner of Lunacy, judges, and army officers. They included seven sisters, a clutch of great great aunts who in middle life decided to go to Zanzibar and bring the word of God as interpreted by high Anglicans to the natives. Aunt Laura in particular became a good friend of the Sultan.

Within days of taking over the house my father planned drastic changes. Once again the dreaded word self-sufficiency was mentioned, and the very first improvement proposed was the dynamo which would harness the waters of the Dargle River. Then the problem of heating had to be tackled.

Unlike most of the houses we had viewed, St Valery, like Farmhill, had an old-fashioned central heating system to keep the members of the religious sect warm as they sang their hymns. As a sop to my mother, my father had the tepid pipes and creaking Victorian radiators overhauled and put in a new boiler. But after a month as we sat in the large dining room my father announced over breakfast.

'Do you know the wretched boiler has already gobbled up more than a ton of coal. We can't afford it.'

He did not relent even during the winter of 1947 when birds fell frozen out of the sky. In time-honoured Big House fashion we hurried from room to room to oases of heat represented by fires whose warmth did not go beyond the hearth rug and paraffin stoves that gave off more smell than warmth. To heat Mr Walker's vast main hall and staircase an anthracite stove was installed which blew out a poisonous cloud of smoke. This was the stuff on which Uncle Paddy had run his car during the war. We ran through the hall holding handkerchiefs to our mouths and noses, and from time to time my mother would go up to the edge of the stove which burned white hot and retrieve a contented dog or cat lying blissfully in the heat unaware it was killing itself. On many mornings a maid would sweep up the corpses of mice.

Mr Walker's light touch with architecture did not reach down to the basement which had the feel of a coal mine with the breathless musty air which is the result of rising damp. The dark semi-underground rooms included the quickly obsolete boiler house and the kitchen, dominated by an Aga. Fed on the same fuel with which we were poisoning ourselves upstairs, it did not leak its fumes in the same way; being Swedish, it had to be good. However, it was just as greedy as the central heating boiler had been. Feed me, feed me, it would demand constantly, and threaten to go into a faint if another hod of anthracite was not poured into its maw. But unlike the people upstairs, the kitchen staff were warm and not threatened with asphyxiation.

The maids and Cook were selected by my father for their ugliness. Any girl with good looks had more chance of getting a boyfriend who would become a husband; and then we would join the lengthening queue of people advertising for plain cooks or household generals. So my father – never my mother – picked out applicants for such positions on the basis of their plain appearance and if they had some little disfigurement so much the better.

Mary was an obvious choice because her squint. She

waited on us up in the dining room. Contact between the kitchen and upstairs was by the lift that brought up food.

'Are ye there?' Lizzie the cook (too old to attract a husband) would roar up the shaft as she put food into the shelves and Mary pulled it up, heaving the rope hand over hand as if she was hauling the mainsail of the *Shira*. It was easy enough to get the serving dishes out and bring them to the big table with fat legs, that had come from Farmhill. The trouble was getting the plates back to the kitchen. The shelves of the lift were not quite true, and Mary's eyesight gave trouble; instead of putting the plates and dishes squarely on the shelf, she would miss and there would be a crash as they failed to connect.

'Oh, dear!'

'Not again!'

Many years later, before we left the house, we inspected the bottom of the lift shaft and found it full of debris, pieces of broken delf from the Masonware plates, a silver teapot which had never been missed, a salt cellar with little claw feet and several bright cut spoons.

In spite of her squint, soon after she came to work for us, Mary received not one marriage proposal, but two. Serve my father right. Having made her choice, she also chose my mother to be her matchmaker.

At St Valery my father had devised a new way of life with a new routine. (But there was always time to go down to the island.) He was rebuilding his medical practice which had gone into abeyance during his long absence and stayed away in Dublin all week, coming down on Fridays for the weekend. There would usually be at least half a dozen guests, since he had continued the practice of inviting people to come and help him work on the place. It was so much easier for them to drive out to Bray than make their way two hundred miles to Illaunslea. Very often the guest workers were doctors, ambitious young housemen who, we were firmly convinced, hoped to advance their careers by pleasing their boss. After a substantial lunch they would be handed spades and forks and shown what work had to be done, and a couple of hours later, sweating and hungry again, they would find teatime awaiting them as a reward.

What a lot of time we wasted at tea in those days – handling pearl-handled cake knives provided by Miss Whiddy, taking barm brack off a silver lotus cake stand with my grandfather and even during the Emergency eating drop scones with Mrs Penrose and Canon Synge. My mother would whip up huge sponge cakes thick as feather mattresses, buttressed by quantities of whipped cream and jam, essential stopgaps before the evening meal.

After the guests had departed, my father would stay on for an hour or so, and then he would leave too. He would load up the car with home-grown vegetables, fruit and flowers and set off for the mews at the back of the garden behind the house and consulting rooms in Fitzwilliam Place which he had converted into a flat.

'It's more convenient.'

My mother had less and less place in his life. The years of loneliness and separation had gone for nothing. We heard rumours – only rumours, nothing was ever discussed – that he had another life altogether. He had grown away from her, as he had from us.

He must have noticed that she was unhappy, and he resolved to do something about the situation in his own way.

One day I noticed a regal black pram with a baby in it parked beside the front steps.

'Who is the baby in the pram?'

'It's your new sister,' said my mother.

I regarded her with astonishment. There had been no mention of babies and anyway she was quite old – approaching fifty. I looked down uneasily at the squirming figure.

'What's her name?'

'Catherine. She's two months old.'

That was one element of the mystery solved; she could hardly be a blood relation. It was hard to work out what had happened, and as usual we had not been consulted. She could have been found in a cabbage patch.

'Is she from the Magdalen?'

'Of course not.'

My mother was still patron of the home for unmarried Protestant mothers and her conversation was full of their woes and problems, However, the issue of even a first fall from the Magdalen would not do for my father. He would only take on the very best sort of baby.

'Where did she come from?'

'Harry arranged things.'

It was only then that I learned how my father's friend, Harry Michael, was responsible for this revolution in our lives. In his role of family doctor Harry had met a wealthy young Englishwoman who was pregnant. This was a serious business in the early 1950s. She and her family considered that to be an unmarried mother in England was a social calamity, and she had decided to come over to Ireland for her confinement and then try and find people who were kindred spirits, wanting to adopt an extremely high-class baby. Harry and my father worked out a solution. One or other of them would adopt the child. Harry and his wife, Rosa, had three daughters and they decided that if it was a boy, he would have it. My father, with his two sons, would take it on if it turned out to be a girl. My mother and Rosa thought this was an excellent idea.

In those days there was no such thing as official adoption in Ireland. There were no papers to sign or annoying social workers to report on whether my eccentric aging parents were suitable for their new role in taking on a young baby. As long as the baby was the same religion as the parents, no one cared and no one would interfere. (A friend of mine was taken to an orphanage to choose a baby brother. 'That one!')

In future years Catherine's favourite bedtime story would be about the arrival of her birth mother in Ireland accompanied by an Alsatian dog. After Catherine was born, her mother and the dog went back to England. Harry had lost his bet and the infant was handed over to my parents in a wicker basket like a puppy.

'If I had been a boy would I have gone to Harry and Rosa?'

'Yes, dear, you are very lucky.'

My mother registered her as her own baby and no questions were asked; this fact would come in useful when Catherine came to need a passport.

Although many years had passed since our own nursery experiences in Fitzwilliam Place, child rearing had changed very little in our family. A wing was installed in St Valery with a large nursery and various other rooms, including a bedroom for an ancient Nanny. This Nanny must have been the last of her kind, and this was her final post. She was a kindly wrinkled old lady, always in a state of bewilderment, and added to the chaos that my mother caused.

'I'm sorry Ma'am, I've burnt the kettle again.'

Plates were always dropped and things got lost, new strap shoes, a length of ribbon and even a dress. 'Where could it have got to?' And she could not deal with the dogs – 'those nuisances' – who stole into the nursery to seize the baby's bottle or a newly opened tin of baby food.

The rest of us lived in the greater part of the house, totally cut off from the nursery. Our own childhood at Fitzwilliam Place was being replayed. Only in the afternoon would Baby appear in her pram, surrounded by furry toys, in a new frilly dress with a smocked yoke down the front.

If it was the weekend my father would be picking her up and holding her in his arms making loving noises. My mother was in heaven, and soon we all shared her enthusiasm. She was a handsome baby with fair hair and brown eyes, and she had a bubbly disposition. She brought us all great happiness. Whether my father truly felt that getting a new baby would make up for lost years and lost love was hard to fathom. I wonder if when he made his plans to adopt Catherine, he already knew that he did not have long to live.

13

My Father's Death

A SPECIAL CAR brought Catherine and Nanny and everything a baby needs down to the island. They were put into Downey's shed, the original island cottage beside the turf shed with its open fire which had once produced loaves of pot oven bread. Even on the island Nanny and her charge were separate from the rest of us. Soon Catherine was on her feet. The hen run with its wire surround was emptied of hens and she was put in it; from there she shouted at us when we went by.

She was too young to go sailing, lucky girl. These days Phil and I were press-ganged into becoming crew on the *Shira*, to haul away at ropes, and heave up the anchor in a shower of black mud.

I remember one particular stormbound anchorage – the harbour of Dungarvan in County Waterford. The *Shira* had its full complement of crew, half a dozen of my father's friends who had been cajoled into making a longer voyage than usual. A ship of fools, buffeted by wind and rolling seas, had gone all around the south coast of Ireland and arrived, as John Betjeman wrote in the refrain of one of his Irish poems, 'In Dugarvan, in the rain'. We could neither land nor sail away.

Momentarily the weather lifted a little and someone was

heard to say. 'I've had enough.' The ship's cook, a Dublin barrister, had spent most of the last three days in the small galley near the anchor chain. He was a broken man.

'It's your decision,' said my father, keeping his feet on the heaving deck, and above the wind we could hear the contempt in his voice. 'Of course, it leaves us short.'

We watched longingly as the plump figure climbed into the dinghy and his stout back got smaller as he was being rowed to Dungarvan and dry land. He was escaping and it was little comfort to us in our misery that he would never be invited on a cruise again. My father's wrath would be turned on him like Pharaoh's; the charm that mesmerized so many of his friends would turn into scorn.

Around this time someone dared to confess to him that they did not really like cruising in total discomfort. There were other reasons why he reluctantly decided to get rid of the *Shira*. There are few relationships closer than that of a yachtsman and his yacht, and the grand old cutter had been the love of his life and prominent in the dreams and memories that he took away with him in wartime. But now the time had come for a parting. During the years when she had been laid up beside the Blackwater she had aged. She had cumbersome old-fashioned rigging, plenty of brass that had to be polished, gleaming teakwood decks to be scrubbed and other luxurious appointments and items of heavy maintenance that were not justified by a few weeks summer sailing. She really needed two paid hands to keep her trim.

She would be replaced by a modern yacht, suitable for the more modified type of day trips my father had in mind. That trip to Dungarvan had been among the least enjoyable he had ever taken, and now he seriously thought of giving up long cruises altogether. (But he had done that before.)

The *Shira* was not easy to sell, being the nautical equivalent of Laragh, and it was many months before some fool took her on. I hope he had good sea legs. While she was being disposed of, my father got to work immediately at designing a new yacht. The *Gannet* would be a smaller, simpler vessel with a large open cockpit and a Parson's engine. No longer would some unfortunate have to climb out to the end of the long bowsprit with a brush to clean the anchor, which would be replaced by the much smaller CQR. A child would be able to do the rigging.

Rather than going to a manufacturer my father built the keel himself – or he got Billy and Miley to do it. From all over Ireland pieces of lead began to arrive at St Valery; broken pipes and scraps accumulated in the yard in a rising heap around which cars and the Ferguson tractor had to negotiate.

He changed into his battle fatigues to supervise Billy as the lead was melted over a large primus and turned it into ingots. Whenever I was available my duty was to fetch the broken pieces and bring them over to the fire for each slow cooking. My father looked on happily.

I went with him regularly into the heart of Dublin to watch the various stages of construction. The shipyard was the last boat-building yard in the city; and when the *Gannet* was completed it would close down. The hull grew week by week. 'She'll take you everywhere you want to go except to the funeral yard,' the builder said, as my father critically examined the rising woodwork.

My saddest memories of this time, and of time past, are

of our frosty relations. We did not learn to love each other, or even work up a basic respect. While teenagers are notoriously difficult, both Phil and I had found our relationship with our father continuously fraught with stumbling blocks. Phil suffered more than I did – ('Peter's a hopeless case!')

Phil was burdened with the prospect of a brilliant future. From time to time influential friends were invited to St Valery for dinner and he would be presented to them – a diplomat, banker or successful businessman. While nothing was spelt out, there was no doubt that my father hoped that the meetings would encourage him to decide his future. I, too, met these people, but I do not think my father believed that I could have a place in their plans.

He placed great hopes on Phil and his brilliance, which proved infinitely harder on my brother than it was on me, since so much was expected of him. There were some conversations on the lines of 'What shall we do with Peter?' and mention of a sugar plantation in South America where someone was also looking for a likely fellow to supervise the Indian workers. Conscious that I was a disappointment, I ignored him or was defiant.

He was either clumsy, as when he approached sex instruction from a purely medical viewpoint, with a lurid description of venereal diseases, or angry when I took no notice of him. We had a terrible row over whether I was going to attend church or not. 'If you don't turn up to Matins, don't bother coming home.' He was furious when I refused to take his advice about the motorbike.

This was soon after he got back from the war. I had saved up and set my heart on a medium 250 CC BSA going cheap.

215

'I really think it's most unwise. I have seen the results of far too many serious accidents involving motorbikes.'

'I want it.'

A week later he handed me a detailed letter filled with statistics of accidents on Irish roads in which motorbikes were involved. It was typical of him that he did not say no but left it to me to make up my own mind. Right away I went and bought it. The subject was never mentioned again, even when I was thundering up and down the avenue at St Valery, and so far as he was concerned I had made my choice. He did not suggest that I should wear a helmet.

I was properly punished. In the summer I took the bike to France, my friend Michael riding behind me. In Paris we decided to spend our last night in a nightclub. The two ladies who joined us at the dimly lit table chose the most expensive sort of drinks and at the end of the evening we had insufficient to pay the bill. Michael spent the rest of the night in a cage with pimps and street walkers while gendarmes accompanied me back to our hotel for the rest of the money. He got out of jail, but we were stony broke.

At least I had the bike, and there was quite a lot of fuel in it. We told ourselves that all we had to do was to bike to Le Havre, and use our boat tickets to England; there we would borrow. Or something. But a few miles outside Paris the main bar holding up the engine broke in two.

After tying up the engine with rope, we had to wheel the wretched heavy machine a hundred and fifty miles. '*Rien! Rien!*' shouted various hotel-keepers as we tried to make bargains about washing up in exchange for food. After the third day we were reduced to stealing into fields and digging up raw potatoes.

Somehow we got back to England and then to Ireland. My father said nothing when he heard. I wonder if he thought much about the bike he himself had when he was very young? He had conducted his courtship on it, taking my mother for rides on the pillion all around County Dublin. Her parents were annoyed, not so much for any idea of hair-raising danger, but because they were old-fashioned and believed that her reputation had been compromised.

At St Valery I used the room in the tower as a study. One warm afternoon as I sat reading in a desultory fashion, outside the window old Bart, the gardener, died. I heard him groan and knew he was dead before I looked out of the window. I waited a few moments and then saw him looking peaceful and at ease with himself in his crumpled old clothes, his hat lying beside him on the grass.

That evening Bart was brought to a back bedroom in the house where we went to pay our respects together with his friends. The small now well-dressed figure on the bed, with his parchment pale face and crossed hands from which trailed rosary beads, was the first dead person I had seen.

In a few months my father would be dead as well. There would be no time for us to become friends.

When he suddenly became ill my mother said, 'He's very tired and needs a good rest.' At once we were frightened, because tiredness was something we had never associated with him.

I visited him in hospital where he had insisted on going to a public rather than a private ward. In this way those who called in to see him would be restricted to visiting hours. From long experience he knew that few things worked more against a patient's comfort than the well-intentioned chatter of friends and relatives.

'Hello, old boy.'

He was sitting up propped against pillows; if a little paler he looked no different – the same dark inquisitorial eyes, the same barely concealed expression of being interrupted in some important work. Miss Spratt, his secretary, sat beside him taking notes.

'I'm trying to work out Iraqi dynasties.' He showed me a paper on which he had listed Amorites, Hittites, Elamites, Kissites and many more. 'You've no idea how complicated these Middle East dynasties can be. Even the experts get them wrong.' He smiled at me. 'It's a wonderful opportunity to get this written up before I go home.'

I loved him then.

When he came out of hospital he seemed smaller and more shrunken and far less intimidating;

'We'll have to stop melting lead for the *Gannet* for the time being.' The scrap metal lay piled up in the yard. The installation of the new dynamo was also abandoned and the great concrete pipes lay in the bottom field.

Our lives continued as if nothing had happened. Every weekend he came home to St Valery, but things were quiet now; the young doctors whom he had put to work stayed away. Instead of the bustle, there was a nightmare quality about each too-quiet weekend, after which he continued to insist on returning to the mews in Dublin, his car filled down with fruit and vegetables.

Then unexpectedly he decided to go down alone to the island.

'I imagine he wants to look at the new boathouse,' my

mother said. I remember thinking how unlike him it was to go down without any of his friends. He did not even stay on the island, but at Lena's guest house in Sneem. He returned like a new man. The guest house had been wonderful, and Lena had entertained him on the piano, singing songs.

We told ourselves that the Kerry air and the spirit of companionship in a place he loved so much was all he needed to get better.

But a week later, when I returned to St Valery from Trinity, my mother said, 'He's not well.' He had had a relapse and was sent over to London to King Edward VII's Hospital for Officers.

Neither Phil nor I had been consulted about the sale of Laragh, or his rift with my mother, or the adoption of Catherine, or even the building of the *Gannet*. Now he did not take us into his confidence about his illness.

I do not remember when he learned that he had leukemia. During the past months he never discussed his illness and all we knew was that something was terribly wrong. Did he feel that worrying the family would only add to the pain?

As a young surgeon he had worked with X-rays in days when people were careless of their fatal content of radium. For twenty years the radium had been stored in his body and now it set out to destroy him.

He was in London for twenty-four days, during which my mother went over three times.

'How's Daddy?'

'Oh, much improved . . . I really think they are getting somewhere.' Did she believe it? 'He's so looking forward to coming home.'

When he came back he had the strange pale look of people who are really ill, and he did not come home to St Valery or see the island again. Near the cottage hospital at Monkstown outside Dublin, where he went to die, was the sea. That April was particularly stormy and a large three-masted sailing ship had been blown off course into the Coal Harbour. Her side had been stove in, her towering masts were splintered, and day after day the gale force winds whipped around her. Every time I visited my father I felt compelled to go down and watch each strong gust tearing her apart.

He would have hated for us to be all around him at his last moments. So he died apart from us and the news came while members of the the family were eating lunch in the Salthill Hotel. When the waitress came in, the telephone message was not for my mother, but for his brother, my Uncle Paddy. Outside the wind rattled the windows and the silver of the sea and breaking waves resounded on the rocks.

I have his death certificate headed by the strangely threatening statement: TO ALTER THIS DOCUMENT IS A SERIOUS OFFENCE. He probably would not be pleased that I know the 'Certified Cause of Death and Duration of Illness' was: 'renal failure 3 months. Sub Mucous Haemorrhages and Acute Myclogenous Leukemia – Certified.' He would consider it none of my business. I have the account from King Edward VII's Hospital for Officers. The bill came to £63. 16s. 1d. I have often thought of that penny.

He was forty-nine when he died, over twenty years younger than I am now. In his short frenetic life, so filled with changing projects dictated by his energy, he did not give himself time to build up a practice. But he is remembered as a brilliant doctor and surgeon. One memorial to him is Cappagh Hospital which his enthusiasm and insistence helped to found.

During our life together I can never remember him mentioning politics. He and his brothers were caught up in the Troubles as schoolboys; afterwards they decided to live in Ireland and for them their Irishness was never in doubt. But they ignored politics and the newly awakened world of nationalism. A minority of Irish people lived happily in their small comfortable beleaguered world. They turned inward on themselves. Some enclosed themselves in cold decaying houses behind estate walls. A few found islands.

When my grandfather was young great pains were taken for people to be taken back and buried among their own people. Our family should all be buried in Cork. And Cork has the lovely places to lie. We have rights to a vault below the stepped beauty of Shandon church, and among Uncle Bris's papers, is a receipt for a grave plot in the cemetery beside St Finbarr's Cathedral, the Gothic dream of William Burges.

However, the family have been away from Cork for a long time and at some point they chose to be buried at Carnalway in Kildare near the comfortable Rectory where my grandfather spent his happiest years with his dear Bessie, three young sons, a succession of dogs, two parrots and his brothers. The road beside it would have been white and dusty when the Silver Stream was first tried out. The little church where my grandfather was rector is lavishly decorated, partly by him, with a jewelled Harry Clarke window and rich mosaics of vine leaves and grapes.

We gathered branches of budding leaves for his coffin. It was daffodil time and huge bunches of daffodils were picked and tied together with embroidery wool.

My mother did not attend the funeral. As the hearse carrying his body crept through the roads and lanes at its funeral pace countrymen crossed themselves and touched their caps. Carnalway is still a lonely silent place. Just outside the churchyard is the mausoleum of the la Touche family where Rose La Touche, John Ruskin's love is buried. Ruskin used to carry a letter from her, pressed between two sheets of gold, over his heart. In her lifetime the wild Rose galloped around nearby Harristown, the La Touche estate, on her cream-coloured pony, Swift, accompanied by her huge dog, Bruno.

Inside the churchyard is the grave of Major Beaumont, who was Master of the Kildares. Ireland is a small place and he was connected to us through our Cousin Daisy, his mother-in-law. After Major Beaumont died, the next week, during the first meet after his funeral his hounds forsook the fox they were chasing and came in here to gather round his grave. My mother liked this story; and perhaps it is fitting that she is buried nearby. So are my uncles, great uncles, and grandfather. And my father is there too. They all lie under gravestones with very detailed inscriptions both on front and back which sum up their lives and achievements. Catherine was reading them recently: 'Everything there but their dental records.'

She was too young to remember him. But she remembers how when he died Nanny threw a towel over her head and keened.

14

Remembering

A FEW MONTHS after my father's death I remember thinking that life for myself and Phil had become easier. The guilt that I felt is still with me.

His death left a vacuum which we filled in our own ways.

I went off travelling. In the 1950s the Oxus was still far distant, and countries that have since been devastated by savage wars had a measure of civilisation which was the result of isolation. It is not easy to convey the magic and promise of travel that still existed then. I was fortunate enough to see many places in a time of innocence before the jet plane, the Kalashnikov and tourism changed the world.

I wonder what my father would have thought about my decision to take up writing as a career. Most probably very little. My family were quite proud of Cousin Edith, principally as co-author of *The Irish RM*, which made them all laugh. But Cousin Edith had fame thrust upon her, and my father and Uncle Paddy considered other writers worthless, apart from Wodehouse. Uncle Paddy thought I was wasting my time. 'Are you looking for copy?' he would say, and we both knew that 'copy' implied a hack writer with a less than serious approach to literature. Anyway literature was unimportant in the scale of human endeavour.

Liberated from my father's demanding presence, my

mother made a totally different life for herself and Catherine. She set out to recreate a world such as Molly Keane described. This world was for Catherine's benefit, and Catherine fitted into it easily in a way her brothers never could. The horse and the pony dominated, and so did the dogs. One of Catherine's earliest parties was a dog's tea party where neighbouring dogs were invited in and sat up at a table with large bones.

The dogs increased in number, some well bred like Roly, Bruin's successor, another Old English sheepdog, old in every sense by now, with rheumy eyes which you could only see if you lifted up his impenetrable fringe. Other aristocrats were the Skelters, two of them, one after another, shivering neurotic Shelties, and the still more neurotic Borzoi. The graceful puppy, like a glamorous version of a greyhound, grew into a crazed short-lived arthritic which had a habit of lying at the drawing room door; you had to step big to get across him, and if you happened to touch him with your foot, he would snap at your calf. King, the Alsatian, was also touched, having suffered a bout of distemper that affected his brain.

When people called in for tea a gust of wind might blow through the open window, tinkling the chandelier, and suddenly the drawing room door would burst open as the guest, having negotiated the Borzoi, made his appearance.

'How lovely to see you!' My mother's words of welcome could hardly be heard against the savage growling.

'Down King! Down Patsy!' And the guest had to pass each Cerberus to take his seat beside the fire.

Considering how gentle my mother was, it was strange that these dogs (Roly was always the exception) were so unreliable in temper. Tradesmen loathed them since the roar of their barking could easily lead to something painful. The postman would run; it hardly mattered if the bills got chewed up, although it was a pity when the brown paper wrapped cylinder containing *Country Life* was gnawed into illegibility. The butcher would leave meat wrapped in white paper on the window sill and also run. Often a dog would be seen with a bloody bone in his mouth which should have been the Sunday dinner. A trail of Haefner's sausages would snake across the lawn. This was in spite of happy hours spent preparing dogs' food, mixing stale bread with meat from a sad bullock's head left in the Aga overnight until the flesh fell away from the skull and the eyes were left still looking reproachful after twelve hours.

Some of the dogs, like Weenie, Patsy Fagan, and Rascal the hen-killer, were strays with pathetic pasts which did not improve their neuroses and tempers. Another stray was the canary that walked up the avenue, knowing that he would find a welcome. My mother put him into a large cage with a cuttlefish and he trilled away happily until she decided that he was lonely and needed a mate. This was a mistake since his new wife henpecked him and he never sang another note after she entered the cage. Outside the peacocks shrieked and the neighbours complained.

My mother was repeating a pattern from the past, remembering how birds had been favourite pets among her relatives up in Derry. Perhaps with their loss of power the Anglo-Irish found it more comforting to turn to birds and animals than men. Birds and beasts couldn't talk back. St Francis might preach to them, but he did not expect a response.

In her childhood home they had kept endless canaries

'detestable birds who were forever getting flu', and a golden oriole which flew around the room during dinner, taking a sip from each glass, on one occasion after a dinner party falling down dead drunk. And there was the old parrot that lived to over a hundred.

In summer time the windows of St Valery would be opened for more animal parties. The white rabbits were allowed into the drawing room and nibbled the Persian carpet, and left their pellets lying around. 'Bad bunnies!' But the droppings were easier to see than the dog messes that mingled with the patterns on the Turkey carpet and missed the Hoover. The drawing room suffered more when the pony came in for tea.

A neighbour complained that the white peacock was responsible for her sister's illness.

'Pure superstition,' said my mother, but she sent flowers from the garden to the funeral. When the cries of the peacocks became too much even for her, they were given away with difficulty – few people wanted them.

For a time St Valery had its resident hermit, a charming deranged lady named Mrs Delaney, generally known as Mad Moll. Mrs Delaney came from a wealthy family who gave her an allowance; she refused to sleep inside. She had glittering green eyes, and tousled knotted hair. She found that the grounds of St Valery suited her, and placed her sleeping bag in a flower bed, coming to the door occasionally for water for tea or to wash with.

'Its not easy when you are camping.'

She was so hardy that in the terrible winter of 1962 she slept outside.

'Beastly weather!' her voice would come from a frozen

bed of leafless roses. But even she did not continue entirely in the ice and snow, and one evening she came inside. She found the only warm room in the house, the dining room, where my mother had succumbed to certain ideas of comfort and installed a coffin-shaped storage heater. She was found sleeping in a wing chair, the heat warmed up her clothes and she gave out a smell like the Great Boo. She did not stay; next day she was away wandering around north Wicklow sleeping in the snowy fields, and opening gates wherever she could since she believed in liberating all the animals in Ireland.

Even without Mrs Delaney there was the usual smell about the place which I always associated with my mother, a medley of dust, flowers, dogs and their doings, and big cold rooms. The atmosphere inside the house could not really be described as sweet disorder. It was more friendly squalor. The shabbiness extended to chipped plates, pieces of broken china and spaces where pictures and pieces of furniture had been sold to passing dealers. The Chelsea shepherd and shepherdess on the chimney piece were armless. In the dining room the gravy boats were bent on their hoofed feet, some making little dancing steps, a legacy of being polished with a heavy hand. They were not polished very much now, since the ugly maids were gone and there was only Mrs Casey to do her best to clean. A small put-upon country woman with an unemployed husband and a quiverful of children Mrs Casey had an air of gentle patience as she went around the house tidying and repairing the untidiness she found everywhere. She was known as Mrs Sisyphus.

Every day she made the house spotless and the kitchen gleam; after she dusted she carefully laid a huge mound of kindling and pieces of coal in the brass fender. Laying the fire in the days before fire lighters was a craft. With luck it would light when evening came without the aid of the double page of the *Irish Times* spread before it, or the paraffin my mother would throw on if everything else failed. Then we could sit down to sherry; since the decanter had lost its stopper, my mother kept a silver tea strainer beside it to sieve out the flies that fell in to a drunken death. The sherry was sipped carefully to avoid the chips on the rim of the battered Waterford glasses which could leave a cut lip and a mouthful of blood. Sherry was the common drink then; it has gone out of fashion and few drink it now, so that the great sherry bodegas in Spain have a quarter of the Irish customers they once supplied.

Like others who once had servants, my mother continued to have her bath at six o'clock in the evening and then change for the dinner she would cook for herself and Catherine – something like baked beans or sardines on toast. The main meal was lunch, cooked and served just after Mrs Casey left at half past twelve By a quarter to one the spotless house would once more be gripped in untidiness. My mother and her dogs moved from room to room leaving devastation behind her, as the kitchen table and floor got covered with spilled flour and cabbage leaves and potato peelings. The chaos in the kitchen became worse during the the course of the afternoon, after she threw together the scones and sponge cake for tea and assembled the dogs' bowls. There were cats as well, not my old cat Prickles, who lived to be twenty and then curled up and died in a moment. These new cats were spoilt and too lazy to get rid of the rats and mice. They were Persian, like Prickles had been, since my mother had a preference for really hairy animals. But little Cushion was the last; no more cats after she crept into the cold oven of the Aga and suffocated; poor braised pussy.

Most departed dogs and cats earned a tombstone. They were easier to bury than horses, which tended to die inconveniently in their stables. When a horse was finally interred with the greatest difficulty on a hillside with a fine view, Billy, our gardener, would compose a song in their honour.

> A fine chestnut steed has gone to his rest
> Of all horses in Wicklow Brandy was the best . . .

Apart from the grief resulting from animal tragedies – the rabbit, the tortoise and from time to time a dog would perish in some drama that caused tears momentarily – I have never seen my mother happier. Where once my father had been the centre of her life, now it was Catherine. There was the air of a perpetual party about St Valery. By the time Catherine was in her teens, horsy friends regarded her house as their house. Teatime produced new guests, the blacksmith, the vet, the whiskery ex-groom, a trainer, ex-jockeys, the stunt man from Ardmore studios, and a youth who told us he was the Thane of Cawdor.

My mother ignored the scoldings from Phil and me and from Uncle Paddy who was in charge of dwindling purse strings.

'You're spoiling the child.'

'Mummy, you shouldn't be doing her homework. The idea is that she should be doing it herself.'

'That dog will have to be put down. One of these days it will seriously hurt someone.'

'Not another saddle! You can't go on buying harness at this rate.'

'Joyce, she's already got two ponies.'

My father had disliked horses and he would never have put up with the horse mania that seized my mother. She had hunted and ridden in point-to-points as a girl, and later had enjoyed the bonanza of horseflesh at Laragh. Now she had Catherine, who from her earliest years proved to be good rider. When at the age of five Catherine was taken to Colonel Hume Dudgeon to learn how, she enjoyed herself, unlike her brothers; under the eye of Sergeant Major MacMaster she would circle the sawdust on Daisy wearing a huge smile on her face.

Money was short and Mr Brennan in his camel-hair coat with the velvet collar, smoking a cigar, came regularly. His introduction was 'I was just motoring by and I thought I'd call in.'

Mr Brennan seemed to be friendly with people we knew who lived in cold houses down the country.

'I was speaking to Mrs Penrose the other day. She is a really nice lady.'

He'd have a table upside down with the speed of an all-in-wrestler.

'I could take that off your hands, Mrs Large.'

'Mr Brennan, we are quite happy with our little table.'

'I know a lady who is looking for something that size, distressed and all.' His eye would twitch as if he shared a secret with her. 'I'll tell you what I'll do.' He would gaze thoughtfully out of the window. 'I'm not pretending the table isn't nice, but they're also quite common.' From the pocket of his coat he would pull out a wad of notes.

'Would you be interested if I gave you a hundred?'

'I don't think so.'

A pause. 'Seeing that you are such a pleasant lady I'll make it a hundred and fifty.'

How did he know that the next financial crisis was due? The bills with their neat lettering and reminders in red were accumulating in the Majolica jar stolen by Uncle Bris and decorated with the arms of the Knights of Malta.

Mr Brennan would pretend to walk away, pause and with the timing of Laurence Olivier would turn his head.

'I could make it two hundred, Ma'am, and that's more than I should spend.'

In five minutes the table would be wrapped in a blanket and put on the roof rack of his station wagon and he would drive away.

'He's not a bad little man,' my mother would say, looking at the visiting card he left behind. 'He tells me he takes Mass every day.'

All over Ireland people in cold houses were seeing their bits and pieces vanishing down their drives, Sheraton and old Irish mahogany on the roof rack, old master paintings and Bossi mantelpieces inside. The money in notes mesmerized them. The father of a friend of mine stripped his drawing room bare at the sight of it.

I was sad about the animal heads and the swords which were slowly vanishing. I never learned what happened to them and suspected an inferior type of Mr Brennan, a traveller, perhaps.

My mother said, 'Some of those heads were mouldy. But I found a good home for the Irish elk horns; I donated them to St Columba's.' She had a vision of them being placed above the portraits of headmasters and the brown pitch pine boards with lists of captains and head boys printed in black paint. Instead the school promptly sold them.

The ivory scenes of torture were still there in the drawing room. I was going to London and undertook to sell them there. The man in Spinks was unimpressed.

'Not everyone's cup of tea.'

There was never enough money now. The envelopes which brought in dividends could not keep pace with the cost of living. There was the dreaded Trust.

'I can't understand why it is impossible to break it,' my mother would say, consigning another bill to the jar. The meetings with accountants, little men, supervised by Uncle Paddy, were depressing occasions.

Uncle Paddy watched over extravagances. 'I can't imagine what he expects me to do.' The new kitchen and the new car were disallowed. My mother would have liked to have kept a racehorse, but was no longer rich enough to consider it. The horse would have been a steeplechaser; she loved steeplechasing. She took us all to Leopardstown, and we watched Arkle, with his loppy ears pricked to the sound of the crowd, winning his race. I wish we had gone to Aintree; nearly every April she had the winner of the Grand National picked, and made a modest profit out of the half-crowns she betted.

As a girl she had loved hunting, but now it was too late for her to return to that pastime. So she enjoyed it vicariously. During the winter Catherine went out with the Bray Harriers, a drag hunt that followed all the routes mentioned in *The Kilruddery Hunt*. Catherine, on Daisy or Shadow, and various children and Dublin doctors and businessmen, would follow Mr O'Brien or his daughter in their green harrier jackets and the scent left in the straw, provided by their tame fox cubs whose unfortunate predecessor had run three hundred years before, over places not yet covered with suburban houses:

> To Carrickmines thence, and to Cherriwood then,
> Steep Shank-hill he clim'd and to Ballyman-glen.

My mother would be in her car, not far behind the steaming horses, and join the convoy of other cars driven by followers, mostly tweedy women all chasing every move of the hunt through mud and rain.

In summer it was showjumping and the horse box travelled all over Ireland. The tack room had essential displays of red rosettes.

'Did you know Brandy got another first?'

Brandy was a showjumper with the potential of an international career. When some fool offered a lot of money I strongly advised disposing of him.

'Sell Brandy! Never!' They cried in unison. It was as if I had suggested selling a favourite slave. In due course he went lame. And then he died and was buried, and Billy wrote his song about him.

> There in the earth under blue Wicklow skies
> A horse of true worth, gallant Brandy lies.

I remember many things about St Valery, the chandelier's dusty garlands, the windows shutting like faulty guillotines, the ambushing draughts, the cobwebs the size of flags blowing leisurely, the mice moving like comets, and the sound of jackdaws in chimneys like rattling tin. I remember the hall, an iceberg to sink the *Titanic*, the black basement and the sitting room with the gilt mirrors and display cabinet filled with broken china, the portrait of my father painted by my friend, David Hone, the Sheraton table carved with his name by Will O'Dea one afternoon as he waited for the telephone, all reflected in the round mirror, topped by an eagle, silver distortion in cracked mercury. Pleasures were there, winter pots of hyacinths and narcissi, roses and summer flowers on dusty tables, smells of roast beef, (barons like the one in Hogarth's picture) sponge cake, and huge fires. And all the animals.

15

Farewell To The Island

O N THE ISLAND the trees planted twenty years ago had become a forest. The coral paths twisted and turned around the headlands: the piers, boathouses and tennis court waited for my father. No yachts now, the *Shira* sold, and the *Gannet*, which my father had not lived to see completed, taken over by Uncle Paddy who preferred to sail her in West Cork.

There was still the familiar sense of delight leaving the mainland, to the splutter from the outboard engine or the groan and thud of oars. Memories were triggered – arriving at night, rowing through the glow-worm shimmer of phosphoresence, smelling mud and seaweed and the dark shape of the island coming nearer. And then my father's voice suddenly calling out, 'Fend off!'

Was that Illaungar, home of a few wary goats, a high silhouette running alongside our own island of Illaunslea?

'What the blazes are you doing?'

I remembered how in the darkness the *Memphis* would pass two or three small inlets around this side, and we would make our way to the pier. At night-time it was always difficult disembarking by torchlight from a boat full of dogs and livestock and luggage, as well as the human cargo.

'Get down, you brute!'

The huge splash would mean that Bruin had jumped into the water followed by the rest of the pack. For dogs and humans alike a sense of triumph awaited on reaching dry land and seeing the dark outlines of the steps and the crane which my father had erected which never worked satisfactorily.

I would leap onto the steps, the slippery painter in my hand.

'Hurry up, Peter.' Pull her in!'

'I don't want a swim at this time of night – I'm already soaking.'

Dinny or Jerry would be waiting with the donkey cart, Dinah appearing indifferent to the drama, her head obstinately down. 'Whoa! Whoa!' Casey or Jerry would make rumbling noises in their throats as Dinah stood still and the cart was filled up. Somewhere in the dark Belinda would be keeping an eye on things. Prickles would be clawing at her basket, the Wyandots and Rhode Island Reds clucking sleepily, and one of the dogs would have bolted howling into the bushes. Eventually the new arrivals, all heavily laden, would start walking up in the darkness under the rhododendron arch, over the coral path towards the house, Dinah following behind.

After the passage over the water there would be a sudden silence, apart from the creak of New Zealand flax being blown by the wind.

'Anything forgotten? Tomorrow it will be low tide.' That meant the *Memphis* would be stuck in the mud until the tide lifted her. The fact that we couldn't get away from the island, even if we wanted, added to the pleasure. That other country, Ireland, had vanished into the night.

Up at the house the turf fire would have been lit and the Tilley lamp hissed softly. Bags, hens, cats, dogs and food were dealt with, school was over and weeks of freedom lay ahead.

My father would be puffing his pipe or smoking a cigarette through an amber holder. My mother would be ticking off choices from a new catalogue of plants, while guests would be searching the bookcase for Agatha Christies. Bruin, who stank after his immersion, would have been banished into the darkness.

'Time for bed, boys.'

In that crowded room, however quiet we kept, we were always spotted and singled out.

'Can't we stay up for a little longer?'

'No.'

We were each handed an oil lamp. It was unfair when we were ten years old. 'Good night everyone.' The ship's ladder led to our bedroom under the eaves and the two bunk beds with their unyielding boards. It never took long to get to sleep.

The light came early through the window that faced east. On the opposite side of the room Phil lay immobile in his bunk. When I looked out towards Rossdohan I could see Jerry rowing across the bay from his house, which was just visible behind him. The boat was a small black dot, gradually increasing in size as he made his way towards the island. After he disembarked I listened to the noise of his boots and then the gurgle of water as he worked the pump. The regular rhythm put me back to sleep.

'Wake up!' Phil was dressed. Downstairs I could hear someone starting the shower and a sudden shout.

'It's perishing cold! Why isn't the water heated?'

Footsteps banged on the boards in the corridor that had once been a ship's deck. Outside sunshine spelt happiness for the day. Above the blue of the Kenmare River the sun lit up the mountains behind Sneem, the bumps and hollows and what they called the Giant's Seat, extending in a great wave.

From the small kitchen there was a smell of bacon where Cook was preparing breakfast. Jerry had finished pumping and was now having his first cup of tea.

'You've got very fat.' Under his peaked cap his weathered face was brown and shining like a chestnut.

My father would be untangling long lines. 'I wish people reeled in their lines correctly when they had finished fishing.'

If the time was after the war he would be wearing the goat-skin trousers he had brought back from Nigeria which creaked like the New Zealand flax. Goat-skin was appropriate for him; the king of another island, Robinson Crusoe, wore goat-skin clothes. Unlike his guests, he would probably have slept well, since he and my mother shared the only room that had reasonable beds. The Skipper's Room, with its low white painted tongue and grooved ceiling, also had the best view, the panorama of the Kenmare River and its islands, the mountains on the south side and the distant hump of Hungry Hill. The quicksilver light changed the view as the clouds moved across the sky.

He liked to spend a happy hour digging into the box of greased spinners, different sized hooks, pairs of spare sails, the CQR anchor and a sextant in its wooden box. If you stepped up and out over the ship's door into the passageway, past the lines of macintoshes and boots and the two little cannon guarding the porch, you might be greeted by a yawning guest who had spent a wretchedly uncomfortable night on one of the bunks. In normal conditions the house could hold about a dozen people, including the maid and cook, but with extra guests it took on the atmosphere of an emigrant ship. Doubling up and squeezing became unpopular words. There were the problems of etiquette about who was next to use the Elsans, inside and out, or to go off and pee discretely into the wet grass.

Breakfast was accompanied by the huge tin pot of tea. So much food passed through the hatch from the kitchen to the large living room. The table had a dumb waiter, made from a bicycle wheel, which circulated boiled eggs, whatever the hens had laid and never enough – first come, first served, except for the boys who had to do without. Never mind, the wheel might also hold sausages and Waterford bacon bought at O'Brien Corkery's, slices of the delicious white bread, made by John O'Shea, the baker in Sneem, jars of home-made marmalade that had been carried over the water in one of the cardboard boxes and, with luck, some of Uncle Paddy's honeycomb. And after a day or two there would always be mackerel.

No one was allowed to mention any particular wish or plan that indicated they wanted to spend their holiday in their own selfish amusement. The plans came from on high. My father made a point of not letting anyone know the day's schedule until the last moment. The barrister and the specialist doctor, who were spending a holiday here that might or might not be enjoyable had no idea of the programme ahead. A remark to Phil or me like 'I wonder could you go to the loft for some sails,' or, 'Have you checked the fishing tackle?' might give an indication for a master plan.

Nothing would happen for the time being and we would

leave my mother supervising the making of sandwiches. Time for a round of the island paths on our bicycles, tearing across the suspension bridge and winding down between the trees to the open spaces at the west end. Or a game and a quarrel on the coral tennis court; around us the fuchsia swarmed with bees.

'That's out!'

'Wasn't!'

'Out! Out! Deuce!'

Whacking balls over a net was a stupid sport. Soon the tennis rackets would be thrown on the grass and we would be touring round our twenty-acre kingdom. I have walked around the island a thousand times, over the same spongy turf paths, seeing the same rocky headlands and catching the smells of seaweed. A gannet diving or oystercatcher taking off and squeaking would make the difference to the circuit; near Illaungar the seals would be laid out or bobbing in the sea. A glimpse of the otter snaking through the seaweed would be a bonus, its tousled head looking as if it used Brylcreem. Was it the same animal every time we saw it, or were there lots of them? At the west end the gulls nested, wheeling, diving and circling above the rocks. Their angry shrieks and the dull thumps of the waves were the only sounds to disturb the profound peace.

Back at the house, while nothing had been said officially, it was generally agreed there would be a sailing party. A day sailing in the sunshine, dogs included, not a proper cruise, not one of the expeditions that ended in agonised entries into the log book. 'Force six. Never again.'

We would pile into the *Memphis* and go over to where the *Shira* sheltered in the lee of Garnish Island, a fine sight with her glistening white hull and truculent bowsprit, her mast topping the surrounding trees. This was the moment the Skipper waited for, the sense of command over lesser mortals. He did not actually turn into Captain Bligh when he was aboard, but there was no doubting who was in charge, and his voice giving orders was clear enough from bow to stern.

The essential was to get away without using the engine which was only for emergencies. The skill of the good yachtsman was to leave or arrive at any anchorage under sail, having given the command of working the capstan to someone else. The *Shira* sported five different sails, including a topsail, and after much heaving of ropes, when she was fully rigged she was a graceful sight against the mountains and the sea.

'Lines out!' Fishing and sailing went together, except when the weather was really bad. Then the mainsail would be lowered and reefed and everything tied down, anchors, boat hooks, canvas buckets and fishing gear. The forward hatch would be closed down, the portholes closed, and the plates and mugs embossed with the *Shira*'s name and a blue anchor would be moved to safety. We would crouch in the cabin, suck Fox's glacier mints or barley sugar, and listen to the groan of timber and the lash of waves as the yacht heeled over and we prepared to be seasick.

But not today, a glorious sail to West Cove, in hot weather, bottom fishing on the way. Forty-five mackerel. The dogs yelping as the *Shira* made the bay, her keel only touching the sand very slightly. The picnic, followed by pollock fishing, rowing around the rocks. 'Fourteen good sized fish. Excellent sport. They appear to stay in shoals. All were caught on the reel in preference to the spinner which was also towed.'

Or another hot day of calm, we might be calling in on

Sherkey, where the oystercatchers shrieked and seals slipped off the rocks as the *Shira* slid into anchor and we claimed the island as our own. Our first priority was the search along the beaches for those luminous glass balls which used to be attached as floats to fishing nets before the advent of plastic. Their narrow range of colours, clear, sea green and bottle green, seemed to link them to seas and oceans. After they were detached from their nets, they would float our way, and especially if there had been a hard winter of storms, up to a dozen might be washed ashore at Sherkey, whose little strands were exposed to the wide mouth of the Kenmare River. They were more prized than Easter eggs and I have many of them still. Afterwards came the search for shells, circus tops, tiny cobalt mussels, some worn to transparency, the thin peeled mother of pearl of ancient oysters, such as once surrounded the Oysterbed Pier, and the occasional prized cowries like the tips of our fingers.

Always a swim in the clear blue freezing water of the bay. One photograph shows me as 'the boy who forgot his bathing suit . . . fully dressed.' I am shown with a wreath of seaweed around my middle.

'It's the turn of the women.'

The spread was laid out, nothing to make a chef dance, ham sandwiches, jam sandwiches, Marmite and limp slices of processed cheese, like Dali's watches, laid on Jacob's cream crackers, fruitcake, chocolate and Roses' lime juice and strong tea. Never another soul on the place. Our task was to collect sticks and sprigs of gorse to add to the strips of news-paper brought along to place in the lining of the Volcano kettle. Slowly it would come to the boil in a hushed moment, like a Japanese tea ceremony.

No humans lived on Sherkey. As we moved over the abandoned fields we lifted hares that so far had escaped the hare hunts and ran before us; thousands of butterflies, peacocks, red admirals and tortoiseshells, hovered over the thistles and clover. And if it was a year when cattle had been swum over to graze among the wild orchids there would be mushrooms, either small and white, scattered by the dozen, or big horse mushrooms, the size of cow pats.

The rocks that bordered Sherkey were a rich enlargement of those on our island, at low tide acres covered with fronds of red seaweed, narrow creeks, and inlets. Before they filled with diamond clear cold water, as the tide came in, we would wander among the rock pools filled with squirrel red sea anemones, looking like little beads above water, and shrimps the size of bananas, and where the water was deeper, the larger sea green snakelocks anemones, a swathe of scallops on the sand, and starfish and red spined sea urchins.

Later there was the return, all the toing and froing to get passengers, dogs and picnic remains back on board before we weighed anchor and sailed back on a following wind, surrounded by gannets, accompanied by porpoises, flicking in mackerel as we tore along. Behind us to the west, where the Kenmare River met the Atlantic, the sun lowered towards the Bull and the Calf.

In the evening, in the living room smelling of turf and fish, we would eat the catch of the day, together with cakes of bread, often brought over by Jerry or Dinny, having been baked in their wives' pot ovens. Afterwards my father would still be restless – if the weather was still fine, there would be time for a game of tennis or an expedition after conger eels or a trip over in the *Memphis* to the Parknasilla Hotel. If it was raining after the meal, he would sit sorting out fishing tackle while the guests amused themselves as best they could, and Leslie Hutchinson sang 'Night and Day' and 'The Nearness of You'.

Only when he was not there did we play cards with my mother and her friends by the light of the Tilley lamp; during the war the young servicemen from Australia and elsewhere would give us a few rounds of Hearts and Racing Demon before they went off to the hotel. After my father died we would stay in and play the new game from America, Canasta. But when he was alive, the daylight hours were never too long, nor the evening or darkness; every minute was precious, as if he knew that he had so much to fit into a short life. I never remember him going to bed.

Phil and I and were out of it in the evenings. Strictly at nine o'clock we said good night reluctantly; we were not allowed to grumble. Then we would take our lamps and go up the ship's ladder. Tomorrow would be another good day.

Some years after my father died I was alone on the island. Day after day the weather was damp and grey – downpours in the morning and a few hours in the evening when the clouds vanished and, when I walked to the west end, the evening sun shone on the raindrops on the straw-covered grass. Near the house the garden was still largely as my mother had created it. Dinny, who came to us in the late 1940s, continued to weed and cut the grass around the Swedish sundial and the pink ridges of rock that led down to the tennis court where weeds had begun to grow among the coral.

When a day dawned without rain, I got the idea of continuing the tradition of improvement. I would make another path.

The lines of paths which crossed the island had been one of the first of my father's projects when he acquired the island a quarter of a century before. One led past the orchard to the coral strand. Another luxuriated in tree ferns, camellias and palms, but you were never taken in by the tropical atmosphere. You might get a day or two of Pacific sun, but sooner or later the woefully damp Kerry air would be back and the Kenmare River, where the clouds gathered all day and moss was growing up the trunks of tree, ceased to be Tahiti.

Another path, lined with fuchsia, looped around the edge of the island, following the contour of ridges to our old Dare Devil Cave and then petered out beside the open sea. Cowland, relatively untouched, had a blend of gorse, royal fern, yellow iris, and a pool in which water lilies burst open in summer. Sea pinks and white campion were bunched on the rocks and the heather had to battle the gales which in autumn and winter roared over our little island, turning the sea smoky, so that the sea spray swept in and covered the house.

You could make a complete circuit past the two creeks and the rocky peninsulas and the places where the winds abated and the rocks would be mirrored in the sea where you could see an image of a heron flying away. But there was one central valley which my father had not exploited. Hemmed in by high ridges of rock, it remained tranquil and unexplored; the holly and trees which had been planted for shelter had thickened to impenetrable jungle. Here I made my first attempts at slashing and uprooting. I planned the finished path, backed by tree ferns, leading straight through from the garden to the open sea.

The ground was sedgy as I scraped back the vegetation, revealing the earth, a rich chocolate brown halfway to turf. Somewhere near here we had buried prime cut salmon and peaches in 1941. I dug, cutting branches, snagging the thick undergrowth, clearing the way and covering the earth with stones and layers of coral. I went over to Garnish and, as Phil and I had done as children, got more tree ferns. I planted them beside the Royal Fern which was beginning to unfurl.

The path took the whole summer to complete. It curved away from the house in the direction of the sea, going through a valley that was new territory. Phil and I had never known this warm defile sheltered from the wind, with the rocks that almost made it a tunnel until, at the west end, it reached the sea and light flooded in.

'Not bad, old boy,' I could hear my father saying, 'but who's going to keep it up?'

Not long after my mother casually mentioned that the island had been sold.

'Who to?'

'I think he's a Dutchman.'

A millionaire has it now, and presumably has put in the amenities that my father considered unnecessary like electricity and running water. The Kenmare River is largely unchanged, and dolphins come in from time to time. Recently I was down at the Oysterbed Pier where a yacht was moored. The people who lived on board had been sailing around the world for seven years.

'We have been to most places – the Greek islands, the West Indies, South America, the Pacific Islands. We have never been anywhere more beautiful than here.'